Old Testament Theology

OLD TESTAMENT THEOLOGY

CANON OR TESTIMONY

Walter Brueggemann

Brevard S. Childs

Fortress Press
Minneapolis

OLD TESTAMENT THEOLOGY
Canon or Testimony

Cover image: Savanah N. Landerholm
Cover design: Photo by Souradeep Biswas on Unsplash

Print ISBN: 978-1-5064-8814-1
eBook ISBN: 978-1-5064-8815-8

Contents

Theology as Canon

Brevard S. Childs

THE PROBLEM OF THE CANON

Bibliography

G. C. **Aalders**, *Oud-Testamentische Kanoniek*, Kampen 1952; P. R. **Ackroyd**, 'The Open Canon', *Colloquium, The Australian and New Zealand Theological Review* 3, Auckland 1970, 279–91; G. W. **Anderson**, 'Canonical and Non-Canonical', *The Cambridge History of the Bible* 1, ed. P. R. Ackroyd and C. F. Evans, Cambridge and New York 1970, 113–59; W. R. **Arnold**, 'Observations on the Origin of Holy Scripture', *JBL* 42, 1923, 1–21; J. P. **Audet**, 'A Hebrew-Aramaic List of Books of the Old Testament in Greek Transcription', *JTS*, NS 1, 1950, 135–54; W. **Bacher**, 'Synagogue, the Great', *JE* 11, 640–43; W. J. **Beecher**, 'The Alleged Triple Canon of the Old Testament', *JBL* 15, 1896, 118–28; P. **Billerbeck**, Der Kanon des Alten Testaments und seine Inspiration', *Kommentar zum Neuen Testament aus Talmud und Midrasch* IV 1, Munich 1928, 415–51; L. **Blau**, 'Bible Canon', *JE* 3, 140–50; J. **Blenkinsopp**, *Prophecy and Canon*, Notre Dame, Ind. 1977; J. **Bloch**, 'Outside Books', *Mordecai M. Kaplan Jubilee Volume*, English Section, New York 1953, 87–108;

reprinted Leiman, *Canon and Masorah* (see below), 202–23; J. S. **Bloch**, *Studien zur Geschichte der Sammlung der althebräischen Literatur*, Breslau 1876; J. **Bonfrère**, 'In totam scripturam sacram praeloquia', *Commentarii in Pentateuchum*, Antwerp 1625, 1–92; K. **Budde**, *Der Kanon des Alten Testaments*, Giessen 1900; F. **Buhl**, *Canon and Text of the Old Testament*, ET Edinburgh and New York 1892. H. von **Campenhausen**, *The Formation of the Christian Bible*, ET Philadelphia and London 1972; J. **Carmignac**, 'Les citations de l'Ancien Testament dans "la Guerre des Fils de Lumière contre les Fils de Ténèbres"', *RB*, 63 1956, 234–60, 375–90; R. E. **Clements**, *Prophecy and Tradition*, Oxford and Philadelphia 1975, 54–7; 'Covenant and Canon in the Old Testament', *Creation, Christ, and Culture. Studies in Honour of T. F. Torrance*, ed. R. W. A. McKinney, Edinburgh 1976, 1–12; Jean **Le Clerc**, *Sentiments de quelques théologiens d'Hollande sur l'Histoire Critique de Vieux Testament*, Amsterdam 1686; R. J. **Coggins**, *Samaritans and Jews: The Origins of Samaritanism Reconsidered*, Oxford and Philadelphia 1975; H. **Corrodi**, *Versuch einer Beleuchtung der Geschichte des jüdischen und christlichen Bibelkanons*, 2 vols. Halle 1792; J. **Cosin**, *A Scholastic History of the Canon of the Holy Scripture*, London 1657, reprinted Oxford 1849; S. **Davidson**, *The Canon of the Bible*, London 1880; L. **Dennefeld**, *Der alttestamentliche Kanon der antiochenischen Schule*, Biblische Studien 14.4, Freiburg 1909; L. **Diestel**, 'Die Kritik des Kanons', *Geschichte des Alten Testamentes in der christlichen Kirche*, Jena 1869, 601–20. A. **Eberharter**, *Der Kanon des Alten Testaments zur Zeit des Ben Sira*, Münster 1911; O. **Eissfeldt**, *The Old Testament: An Introduction*, Oxford and New York 1965, 560–71; I. H. **Eybers**, 'Some Light on the Canon of the Qumran Sect', *OuTWP* 1962, 1–14, reprinted Leiman, *Canon and Masorah*, 23–36; 'Some Remarks about the Canon of the Old Testament', *Theologia Evangelica* 8, Pretoria 1975, 88–117; L. **Finkelstein**, 'The Maxim of the Anshe Keneset Ha-Gedolah', *JBL*, 59, 1940, 455–69; E. **Flesseman-van Leer**, 'Prinzipien der Sammlung und Ausscheidung bei der Bildung des Kanons', *ZTK* 61, 1964, 404–20; D. N. **Freedman**, 'The Law and the Prophets', *SVT* 9, 1962, 250–65, reprinted Leiman, *Canon and Masorah*, 5–20; 'Canon of the Old Testament', *IDB Suppl*, 130–6; J. **Fuerst**, *Der Kanon des Alten Testaments nach den Überlieferungen in Talmud und Midrasch*, Leipzig 1868; A. **Geiger**, 'Warum gehört das Buch Sirach zu den Apokryphen?', *ZD MG* 12, 1858, 536–43; L. **Ginzberg**, 'Some Observations on the Attitude of the Synagogue toward Apocalyptic Writings', *JBL* 41, 1922, 115–36, reprinted Leiman, *Canon and Masorah*, 142–63; H. **Graetz**, 'Der Abschluss des Kanons des Alten Testaments', *MGWJ* 35, 1886, 281–98; W. H. **Green**, *General Introduction to the Old Testament: The Canon*, New York

1905; D. E. **Groh**, 'Hans von Campenhausen on Canon', *Interp* 28, 1974, 331–43; H. A. C. **Hävemick**, *A General Historico-Critical Introduction to the Old Testament*, ET Edinburgh 1852, 17ff.; W. W. **Hallo**, 'New Viewpoints on Cuneiform Literature', *IEJ* 12, 1962, 13–26; M. **Haran**, 'Problems of the Canonization of Scripture' (Hebrew), *Tarbiz* 25, Jerusalem 1955–56, 245–71; G. **Hölscher**, *Kanonisch und Apokryph*, Leipzig 1905. E. **Jacob**, 'Principe canonique et formation de l'Ancien Testament', *SVT* 28, 1975, 101–22; A. **Jepsen**, 'Kanon und Text des Alten Testaments', *TLZ* 74, 1949, 65–74; 'Zur Kanongeschichte des Alten Testaments', *ZAW* 71, 1959, 114–36; 'Sammlung und Kanonisierung des Alten Testaments', *RGG*³ 1, 1123–25; A. **Jolles**, *Einfache Formen*, Darmstadt ²1958, 26–8; P. **Katz**, 'The Old Testament Canon in Palestine and Alexandria', *ZNW* 47, 1956, 191–217, reprinted Leiman, *Canon and Masorah*, 72–98; M. G. **Kline**, *The Structure of Biblical Authority*, Grand Rapids, rev. ed. 1972; E. **Koenig**, *Kanon und Apokryphen*, Gütersloh 1917; J. L. **Koole**, *Het Probleem van de Canonisatie van het Oude Testament*, Kampen 1955; S. **Krauss**, 'The Great Synod', *JQR* 1, 1898, 347–77; A. **Kuenen**, 'Über die Männer der grossen Synagoge', 1876, German tr. *Gesammelte Abhandlungen zur biblischen Wissenschaft von Dr Abraham Kuenen*, Freiburg 1894, 125–69; W. G. **Lambert**, 'Ancestors, Authors and Canonicity', *JCS* 11, 1957, 1–14; J. C. H. **Lebram**, 'Aspekte der alttestamentlichen Kanonbildung', *VT* 18, 1968, 173—89; Sid Z. **Leiman**, ed., *The Canon and Masorah of the Hebrew Bible*, New York 1974; *The Canonization of Hebrew Scripture*, Hamden, Conn. 1976; J. **Leipoldt**, *Geschichte des neutestamentlichen Kanons*, 2 vols. Leipzig 1907; R. C. **Leonard**, *The Origin of Canonicity in the Old Testament*, Diss. Boston University 1972; Elias **Levita**, *The Massoreth ha-Massoreth*, trans. C. D. Ginsberg, 1867, reprinted New York 1968; J. P. **Lewis**, 'What Do We Mean by Jabneh?' *Journal of Bible and Religion* 32, Boston, Mass. 1964, 125–32, reprinted Leiman, *Canon and Masorah*, 254–61; A. **Loisy**, *Histoire du canon de l'Ancien Testament*, Paris 1890. H. **Mantel**, 'The Nature of the Great Synagogue', *HTR* 60, 1967, 75–83; M. **Margolis**, *The Hebrew Scriptures in the Making*, Philadelphia 1922; R. **Meyer**, 'Kanonisch und Apokryph im Judentum', *TWNT* 3, 979–87 = *TDNT* 3, 978–87; F. **Michaéli**, 'A propos du Canon de l'Ancien Testament', *Etudes Théologiques et Religieuses* 36, Montpellier 1961, 61–81; G. F. **Moore**, 'The Definition of the Jewish Canon and the Repudiation of Christian Scriptures', *C. A. Briggs Testimonial (Essays in Modern Theology)*, New York 1911, 99–125, reprinted Leiman, *Canon and Masorah*, 115–41; R. E. **Murphy**, A. C. **Sundberg** and S. **Sandmel**, 'A Symposium on the Canon of Scripture', *CBQ* 28, 1966, 189–207; H. **Oppel**, *Κανών, Zur*

Bedeutungsgeschichte des Wortes und seiner lateinischen Entsprechungen, regulanorma, Philologus, Supplementband 30.IV, Leipzig 1937; H. M. **Orlinsky**, 'The Canonization of the Bible and the Exclusion of the Apocrypha', *Essays in Biblical Culture and Bible Translation*, New York 1974, 257–86; G. **Östborn**, *Cult and Canon: A Study in the Canonization of the Old Testament*, Uppsala 1950; R. H. **Pfeiffer**, 'The Canon of the Old Testament', *IDB* I, 498–520; J. D. **Purvis**, *The Samaritan Pentateuch and the Origin of the Samaritan Sect*, HSM 2, 1968; E. W. E. **Reuss**, *History of the Canon of the Holy Scriptures in the Christian Church*, ET London and New York [2]1891; B. J. **Roberts**, 'The Old Testament Canon: A Suggestion', *BJRL* 46, 1963–64, 164–78; J. **Ruwet**, Les Apocryphes dans l'oeuvre d'Origène', *Bibl* 23, 1942, 18–43; 24, 1943, 18–58; 25, 1944, 143–66; 'Clément d'Alexandrie Canon des Écritures et apocryphes', *Bibl* 29, 1948, 240–71; H. E. **Ryle**, *The Canon of the Old Testament*, London 1892. J. A. **Sanders**, 'Cave 11 Surprises and the Question of Canon', *McCormick Quarterly* 21, Chicago 1968, 284–98; *Torah and Canon*, Philadelphia 1972; 'Adaptable for Life: The Nature and Function of Canon', *Magnolia Dei. Essays on the Bible and Archaeology in Memory of G. Ernest Wright*, Garden City, N.Y. 1976, 531–60; 'Hermeneutics', *IDB Suppl*, 402–7; N. M. **Sarna**, 'The Order of the Books', *Studies in Jewish Bibliography, History, and Literature in Honor of J. Edward Kiev*, ed. C. Berlin, New York 1971, 407–13; 'Bible: Canon', *EJ* 4, 816–32; C. F. **Schmid**, *Historia antiqua et vindicatio canonis sacri veteris novique testamenti, libris II comprehensa*, Leipzig 1775; I. L. **Seeligmann**, 'Voraussetzungen des Midraschexegese', *SVT* 1, 1953, 150–1; J. S. **Semler**, *Abhandlung von freier Uniersuchung des Canon*, 4 vols., Haile 1771–75; L. H. **Silberman**, 'The Making of the Old Testament Canon', in C. M. Laymon, ed., *The Interpreter's One-Volume Commentary on the Bible*, Nashville 1971, 1209–15; Richard **Simon**, *Histoire critique du Vieux Testament*, Rotterdam 1685, reprinted, Frankfurt 1967; Morton **Smith**, *Palestinian Parties and Politics That Shaped the Old Testament*, New York and London 1971; W. Robertson **Smith**, *The Old Testament in the Jewish Church*, 1881, London and New York [2]1892; H. L. **Strack**, 'Kanon des Alten Testaments', *RE*[3] 9, 741–68; M. **Stuart**, *Critical History and Defence of the Old Testament Canon*, Andover, Mass. 1845, London 1849; A. C. **Sundberg**, *The Old Testament of the Early Church*, Cambridge, Mass., and London 1964; 'The "Old Testament": A Christian Canon', *CBQ* 30, 1968, 143–55; T. N. **Swanson**, *The Closing of the Collection of Holy Scriptures: A Study in the History of the Canonization of the Old Testament*, Diss. Vanderbilt University 1970; H. B. **Swete**, 'Order of the Books in Jewish Lists', *Introduction to the Old Testament in Greek*, Cambridge [2]1914, reprinted New York 1968, 200. G. M. **Tucker**, 'Prophetic Superscriptions and the Growth of a Canon', in *Canon and Authority*, ed. G. W. Coats and B. O. Long, Philadelphia 1977, 56–70; J. C. **Turro** and R. E. **Brown**, 'Canonicity', *The Jerome Biblical Commentary*, Englewood Cliffs, N.J. 1969, **II**, 515–34; B. F. **Westcott**, *On the Canon of the New Testament*, London 71896; W. M. L. **de Wette**, *A Critical and Historical Introduction to the Canonical Scriptures of the Old Testament*, 2 vols., ET Boston, Mass. 1843; G. **Wildeboer**, *The Origin of the Canon of the Old Testament*, ET London 1895; R. D. **Wilson**, 'The Book of Daniel and the Canon', *PTR* 13, 1915, 352–408, reprinted *Studies in the Book of Daniel*, 2nd series, New York 1938, 9–64; L. B. **Wolfenson**, 'Implications of the Place of the Book of Ruth', *HUCA* 1, 1924, 177f.; T. **Zahn**, 'Zählungen der biblischen Bücher', *Geschichte des neutestamentlichen Kanons* II.1, Erlangen/Leipzig 1890, 318ff.; S. **Zeitlin**, 'An Historical Study of the Canonization of the Hebrew Scriptures', *PAAJR* 3, 1931–32, reprinted Leiman, *Canon and Masorah*, 164–99.

Terminology

The initial difficulty in discussing the issue of the canon arises from the ambiguity of the terminology. What is meant by 'the canon'? The philological evidence for the Greek cognates has often been rehearsed (cf. B. F. Westcott, 513ff.; H. W. Beyer, 'κανών' *TWNT* 3, 613–20 = *TDNT* 3, 596–602). The original meaning of the noun in classical Greek is that of 'straight rod' or 'ruler', which also received a metaphorical sense of rule or norm. The word appears in the LXX and in two passages in the New Testament (Gal. 6.16; II Cor. 10.13–16) with a similar range of meaning which extends from a literal to a more metaphorical, abstract connotation. Among the church fathers the term canon was used in a variety of combinations—'rule of truth', 'rule of faith'—as a norm of church doctrine and practice. Although Origen used the term in an adjectival sense of *scripturae canonicae* (*De princ.* IV 33), the first application of the noun to the collection of holy scriptures appears in the last part of the fourth century and continued in common use from the time of Jerome.

The use of the term canon to describe the scriptures was of Christian origin and not applied in classic Jewish literature. Rather, the rabbis spoke of 'sacred writings' (*kitbê haqqōdeš*) which were said to 'defile the hands' (*metamme'îm 'et-hayyādayim*). Nevertheless, the rabbinic concept has enough in common with the Christian usage for Jews usually not to hesitate to apply the term canon to their scriptures (cf. Leiman; however, cf. the restrictions of L. B. Wolfenson, 177f., and my final chapter).

The real problem of defining the term canon is far from settled by the philological evidence. One needs only a cursory look at the history of interpretation to see immediately how different have been the concepts of canon which have been held over the centuries. Josephus' view of canon (*Contra Apionem* I, 42f.) implies a concept of divinely inspired writings, fixed in number, originating within a limited period of time, with an established text. A somewhat similar definition is reflected in the midrashim (cf. *Bemidbar Rabbah* 14.4), but it also seems clear that the Talmud allowed for different categories of canonical books, and that inspiration and canonicity were carefully distinguished (cf. Leiman, *Canonization*, 127ff.).

Semler argued that such traditional definitions of the canon were later theological constructions and that originally the canon simply designated a list of books which were to be read in open assembly. The term did not imply any particular quality of divine inspiration, nor was there a fixed number of books agreed upon by a consensus. Several recent writers (Sundberg, Swanson) have sought to distinguish sharply between scripture and the canon. They argue that the term scripture designates a body of authoritative writings whereas the canon involves the essential element of restriction and implies a closed collection to which nothing more can be added. Finally, there are those who would project the term canon into the early stage of the literature's formation and define canonization as any act of official publication of a document which achieved a normative status (Freedman, Leiman).

In sum, much of the present confusion over the problem of the canon turns on the failure to reach an agreement regarding the terminology. As a result, the points of both consensus and conflict have been frequently obscured within the debate.

The Traditional View of the Canon and Its Demise

The Old Testament does not address directly the issue of when and how the history of canonization took place, yet various Jewish traditions developed during the Hellenistic period which were accepted by both Jews and Christians at least until the seventeenth century. II Esdras 14.44 (c. AD 100) recounts that Ezra restored in forty days the sacred books which had been destroyed by the Babylonians by his being supernaturally empowered to recall the entire scriptures. The account in II Macc. 2.13 attributes the collection of the sacred writings to Nehemiah. Although the Babylonian Talmud in a famous passage (Baba Bathra 14b–15a) had sought to ascribe authorship to the various books of the Bible, it was Elias Levita who developed the theory of the men of the Great Synagogue under Ezra as having established the canon of the Hebrew Bible and divided it into three parts. This theory was widely accepted by Jews and Christians until the end of the nineteenth century.

In spite of the variations within these traditional viewpoints, they all shared an underlying assumption of an unbroken continuity, even if threatened at times, between the writing and collecting of an authoritative body of scripture. The canon was formed and enlarged as each new book was added. When the last book appeared, the canon was closed. The canon assured an unbroken series of sacred annals which had been preserved from the time of Moses. The establishment of authorship maintained its authenticity, the divine inspiration its truth, the uninterrupted succession its purity.

The collapse of the traditional understanding of the canon was the result of attacks from several directions. First of all, the discovery of a complex historical development of the literature, especially the Pentateuch, seriously damaged the idea of a direct, unbroken link between the original writing and its final stage in which the book's authority had been accepted from its inception. Again, the recognition of a long prehistory raised serious questions respecting the traditional authorship, and thus threatened the canon's authenticity. Then again, the discovery that certain of the biblical books, especially Daniel, probably derived from a period after the alleged closing of the canon under Ezra's leadership did much to question the accuracy of the traditional concept of the canon's history. Kuenen's devastatingly negative judgment regarding the history of the Great Synagogue removed the last foundation block of the older view and wiped the slate clear for a new interpretation.

The Nineteenth-Century Historical Consensus and Its Erosion

The development of a new critical theory of the canon from a strictly historical perspective had been attempted by Eichhorn, Corrodi, de Wette, and others. The varying models suggest that they did not succeed in achieving a wide consensus, chiefly because of the disagreement over the history of the literature. However, with the growing hegemony of Wellhausen's reconstruction of Israel's history and literature, a new consensus began to emerge also regarding the history of the canon. It is reflected in several Introductions (e.g. W. R. Smith, Cornill), in important encyclopaedia articles (Strack), and in the popular handbooks of Wildeboer, Buhl, and Ryle. In spite of some modification the classic literary critical construction of the formation of the canon has continued to be represented in the Introductions of Pfeiffer, Bentzen, and Eissfeldt. The theory agreed on certain main lines of the development.

The Josianic reform of 621 BC, reported in II Kings 22, marked the first step in the process by the canonization of Deuteronomy or some portion of it. At the end of the fifth century in the period of Ezra the Torah had assumed its fixed canonical status with the addition of the Priestly source to the earlier Pentateuchal strands. The dating of the formation of the Pentateuch was established to some extent by the Samaritan schism which marked a *terminus* by which time these books had been set. The prophetic books were next canonized in the third century, and the collection had been firmly closed before the book of Daniel was composed, about 165. The final stage of canonization was assigned to decisions at the Council of Jamnia (c. AD 90) at which time books in use among the Alexandrian Jews were also excluded.

Within the last two decades this classic nineteenth-century reconstruction of the history of the canon has been seriously eroded in several ways. In the first place, most of the fixed historical points upon which the theory had been built seem no longer able to bear the weight placed upon them. For example, recent research into the Samaritan question (Purvis, Coggins) has raised serious doubts whether one can any longer speak of a single event in the fifth or fourth century—the exact date was never settled—which resulted in the Samaritan schism. Nor can the restriction of the Samaritan scriptures to the Pentateuch be used as a *terminus ad quem* for the closing of the first part of the Hebrew canon. Similarly, the argument for the dating of the closing of the final section of the Hebrew Bible by the Council of Jamnia rests on the flimsiest possible evidence. Not only is next to nothing known about this 'council', but what transpired did not relate directly to the closing of the canon. Then again, the research of A. C. Sundberg has successfully destroyed the widespread theory of an Alexandrian canon and seriously damaged the assumption of parallel canons, one narrow and one broad, which were held by different geographical communities within Judaism.

In the second place, the assumption that the Masoretic division of a tripartite canon was the original order reflecting three historical stages in the canon's development, and that the Septuagint's order was a later, secondary adjustment, has been questioned from several sides. Hölscher, Katz, and Lebram have demonstrated the antiquity of other non-Masoretic orders. Margolis (70ff.) has argued for the co-existence of Torah, prophecy, and wisdom throughout Israel's literary and religious history. This approach to canon has tended to sustain the older conservative argument (e.g. R. D. Wilson) that Daniel's exclusion from the prophets in the Masoretic order entailed a theological as much as a historical judgment. One cannot assume that one canonical section was tightly closed before another was formed because of the lack of solid evidence from which to draw such a conclusion.

Finally, the recovery of a sense of oral tradition which criticized the older literary critical school for identifying the age of the material within a book with its literary fixation has also had a damaging effect on the classic critical reconstruction of the canon. Even if one could identify the book which was discovered in 621 (II Kings 22) with Deuteronomy, as most scholars do, it does not follow that one can infer that this event constituted the first stage of canonization of Deuteronomy nor that the laws of Moses were without authority up to that point in history. Many of the same assumptions can be questioned regarding the final stage of the Pentateuch's alleged canonization under Ezra resulting from the addition of the Priestly source according to the classic Wellhausen theory. To extrapolate a history of canonization from a highly complex and obscure literary process remains a very fragile and tentative enterprise.

The Search for a New Consensus

In the light of this erosion in the classic critical reconstruction, a variety of newer attempts have emerged in recent years in an effort to form a new synthesis. Certain characteristic moves can be sketched without attempting to present an exhaustive review of all the literature.

(i) G. Hölscher argued in *Kanonisch und Apokryph* (1905) for a sharp distinction to be made between the growth of the collection of Hebrew writings and the development of the concept of canon. The former was a literary process, the latter a dogmatic theory. Taking Josephus' understanding of canon as representative of the dogmatic canonical formulation, Hölscher argued against seeing a three-stage historical development of the canon. Neither the collection of the Law nor the Prophets was canonical in the strict sense of the term even by the time of Sirach's grandson (c. 130 BC). Rather, the concept of the canon as a dogmatic theory was a product of rabbinic Pharisaism from the time of Hillel and Shammai, which sought to preserve rabbinic tradition by limiting the canonical scripture to a particular period of the ancient past and thus eliminating the new threat arising from apocalyptic writings. The Alexandrian form of the canon with twenty-two books, which counted Ruth with Judges and Lamentations with Jeremiah, preserved the older order of the canon, and only later did Palestinian Judaism change the form to adopt the present Hebrew canon, which contains twenty-four books.

In my judgment, Hölscher made an important contribution in challenging the assumption of the nineteenth-century literary critical school that the three-stage division was the key to the historical understanding of the canon. Also his defence of the priority of the tradition of twenty-two books was impressive. However, the application of a very limited interpretation of the term canon prejudiced the discussion from the outset. By adopting a late rabbinic definition of the canon he failed to explain the forces which led to the collection of these writings and their authoritative function which lay behind the final rabbinical form.

(ii) Almost the exact opposite thesis was proposed by David Noel Freedman (*IDB Suppl*), who argued that the Law and the Former Prophets comprised a literary unit and were compiled and published with some form of canonical status by 550 BC. A 'second edition' which included the Latter Prophets appeared some fifty years later. Freedman claimed that these were public documents promulgated by an 'official ecclesiastical group in the Jewish community' (*SVT* 1962, 251). He assumed that any given writing arose as a response to a specific historical circumstance in the life of the people, and could be dated very close to the last event mentioned in the document. Furthermore, he worked on the assumption that to establish the date in which a writing was given a finished form also established the date of canonization, which he understood as an official promulgation of a public document. In my opinion, none of these assumptions can be sustained by historical evidence; in fact I regard them as highly unlikely. By simply identifying the history of the literature's growth with the history of canonization Freedman has closed off any chance of understanding the special history of the book's growth and collection as canonical scripture which is the very issue at stake.

(iii) Sid Z. Leiman begins his history of the formation of the canon with a clear definition of his understanding of the term: 'A canonical book is a book accepted by Jews as authoritative for religious practice and/or doctrine, and whose authority is binding upon the Jewish people for all generations' (*Canonization*, 14). Leiman then distinguishes between uncanonical writings referred to in the Hebrew Bible and canonical writings.

Using such verses as Ex. 24.7; I Kings 2.3; II Kings 14.6, Leiman concludes that the biblical text is unequivocal: 'The canonization of the Covenant Code, the Decalogue, Deuteronomy, and perhaps the entire Torah is assumed to have occurred during the lifetime of Moses' (20).

In my judgment, Leiman has made a valuable contribution in showing the early age at which documents, particularly laws, exerted an authoritative role. The history of the canon did not start in 621 BC as if the book of Deuteronomy, which had previously been regarded as among the profane writings, was suddenly deemed authoritative. Also Leiman's discussion of the rabbinic evidence for the closing of the canon is of great value. Nevertheless, there are some problems with Leiman's full proposal, in my opinion. Because he makes no real distinction between a book's authority and its canonicity, the entire Pentateuch is assumed to have been canonized during the period of Moses. But then this portrayal of the canonization process fails to reckon with the very history of the literature's development, the recognition of which caused the collapse of the traditional position. Leiman makes a passing reference to Albright's demonstration that ancient tradition has been preserved in the various sources as evidence against the classic literary critical reconstruction. But he still does not make room for the complex history of the literature's growth. Nor does he adequately deal with a history of accommodating, collecting, and ordering of saga and legends stemming from non-Israelite sources which entered the Pentateuch. In the end, Leiman's reconstruction of the history still seeks to defend an unbroken succession of authoritative, canonical writings from Moses to the close of the canon.

(iv) A similar hypothesis, but considerably more apologetic, has been proposed by M. G. Kline, who attempts to establish an unbroken canonical continuity from the Mosaic period by finding an analogy in the ancient Near Eastern suzerainty treaties.

However, Kline's basically dogmatic formulation of the history of the canon in terms of a divine inspiration which assured an inerrant transmission of the Word of God (23) reflects completely the pre-Semler, seventeenth-century understanding which has not even seen the historical problem. These issues are far too complex simply to circumscribe by a strictly theological definition. Therefore, in spite of some excellent insights, the total impact of the book misses its intended goal.

(v) At the other end of the spectrum is the bold attempt of James A. Sanders to reinterpret the history of the canon as an ongoing hermeneutical process extending throughout Israel's entire history. Sanders greatly broadens the definition of the canon to describe the community's attempt to discover its self-identity in the light of its authoritative traditions which it continually reinterprets to meet the changing historical conditions of its existence. According to his model, 'it is the nature of canon to be both stable and adaptable' ('Hermeneutics', 404). It is stable in the sense of having an established structure and content; it is adaptable in addressing the community in each new generation. Although Sanders has not yet worked out the effect of his hermeneutical approach in detail on the entire history of the canonical process, he has drawn some of the broad lines in his book *Torah and Canon*.

In my judgment, Sanders has moved in the right direction in broadening the definition of canon to cover a process extending throughout Israel's history which effected the shaping of the literature itself. However, I am critical of Sanders' existential categories which understand the growth of canon as a search for identity in times of crisis, oscillating between the two poles of stability and adaptability. In my opinion, the historical and theological forces which evoked the formation of the canon were of a very different order from an identity crisis. Nor is the effect of canon on the

literature adequately described by Sanders' category of 'monotheis-
tic pluralism', as I shall attempt to demonstrate in the detailed analysis of each biblical book. Finally, I am critical of Sanders' attempt
to reconstruct the hermeneutical process within ancient Israel,
which appears to be a highly speculative enterprise, especially in
the light of the almost total lack of information regarding the history of canonization. He assumes a knowledge of the canonical
process from which he extrapolates a hermeneutic without demon-
strating, in my opinion, solid evidence for his reconstruction.

To summarize: the task of assessing the role of the canon in
understanding the Old Testament has proven to be an enormously
difficult problem. Its terminology, history, and function remain
highly controversial. In spite of the serious erosion in the classic literary critical reconstruction of the history of canon which emerged
at the end of the nineteenth century, no fully satisfactory new interpretation has been able to achieve a consensus.

A New Attempt at Understanding Canon

It is necessary at the outset to settle on a definition of the term
canon. The difficulty of the subject and its complex historical usage
should caution against too quickly claiming the exclusive right for
any one definition. It is important that the use of the term does justice to all the dimensions of the issue without prematurely resolv-
ing problems merely by definition. One should also expect a degree
of consistency in the application of the term.

The term canon has both a historical and a theological dimension. The formation of the canon of Hebrew scriptures developed in a historical process, some lines of which can be accurately
described by the historian. Semler was certainly right in contesting
an exclusively theological definition of canon in which the element
of development was subsumed under the category of divine Prov-
idence or *Heilsgeschichte* of some sort. Conversely, the formation

of the canon involved a process of theological reflection within Israel arising from the impact which certain writings continued to exert upon the community through their religious use. To seek to explain the historical process leading toward the formation of the canon solely through sociological, political, or economic forces prejudices the investigation from the start.

In recent years there has been a strong insistence from such scholars as Sundberg and Swanson that a clear distinction be made between scripture and canon. Accordingly, scripture is defined as authoritative writings, whereas the canon is restricted to a dogmatic decision through which the limits of scripture are defined and fixed. There are certain obvious merits in making a sharp distinction between the authority of a writing and its canonization. I have earlier criticized Leiman's reconstruction for too easily identifying scriptural authority and canonization, with the result that the complex history of collecting and ordering of a corpus of sacred writings is inadequately treated.

However, there are also serious problems involved in too sharply separating the two concepts after the model of Sundberg and Swanson. First of all, to conceive of canon mainly as a dogmatic decision regarding its scope is to overestimate one feature within the process which is by no means constitutive of canon. It is still semantically meaningful to speak of an 'open canon'. Secondly, the sharp distinction obscures some of the most important features in the development of the canon by limiting the term only to the final stages of a long and complex process which had already started in the pre-exilic period. Essential to understanding the growth of the canon is to see this interaction between a developing corpus of authoritative literature and the community which treasured it. The authoritative Word gave the community its form and content in obedience to the divine imperative, yet conversely the reception of the authoritative tradition by its hearers gave shape to the same writings through a historical and theological process of selecting, collecting, and ordering. The formation of the canon was not a late extrinsic validation of a corpus of writings, but involved a series of decisions deeply affecting the shape of the books. Although it is possible to distinguish different phases within the canonical process—the term canonization would then be reserved for the final fixing of the limits of scripture—the earlier decisions were not qualitatively different from the later. When scripture and canon are too sharply distinguished, the essential element in the process is easily lost.

Part of the difficulty of defining the canonical process turns on the model one uses by which to interpret this history. Although Sanders also understands canon in terms of a dynamic process, we differ markedly in our descriptions of this history. For Sanders the heart of the canonical process lay in Israel's search for identity. In my judgment, this approach turns the canonical process on its head by couching a basically theological move in anthropological terms. It thus replaces a theocentric understanding of divine revelation with an existential history. Indeed, canon involved a response on Israel's part in receiving the authoritative tradition, but the response to a continuing experience with God was testified to by a new understanding of scripture. Israel did not testify to its own self-understanding, but by means of a canon bore witness to the divine source of its life. The clearest evidence for this position is found in the consistent manner in which the identity of the canonical editors has been consciously obscured, and the only signs of an ongoing history are found in the multi-layered text of scripture itself. The shape of the canon directs the reader's attention to the sacred writings rather than to their editors. Israel's own self-understanding was never accorded a place of autonomy, but was always interpreted in the light of the authority of scripture. Because the process of forming the scriptures came to an end, canon marked off a fixed body of writings as normative for the community rather than attributing authority to the process itself. When Israel later reinterpreted its scriptures to address changing needs, it did so in the form of the targum, that is to say, commentary, which was set apart sharply from the received sacred text of scripture.

There is one final point to make respecting the nature of the canonical process. Seeligmann has described a process of interpretation within scripture which he correctly derived from a consciousness of canon (*Kanonbewusstsein*). This process involved the skilful use of literary techniques, word-plays, and proto-midrashic exegesis which emerged during the final stages of the formation of the canon and continued to be developed and to flower during the post-biblical period. Although such exegetical activity grew out of a concept of the canon as an established body of sacred writings, it is a derivative phenomenon which does not represent the constitutive force lying behind the actual canonical process. Rather, the decisive force at work in the formation of the canon emerged in the transmission of a divine word in such a form as to lay authoritative claim upon the successive generations.

The growth of Israel's canon consciousness can be clearly detected when the words of a prophet which were directed to a specific group in a particular historical situation were recognized as having an authority apart from their original use, and were preserved for their own integrity (cf. Isa. 8.16f.). The heart of the canonical process lay in transmitting and ordering the authoritative tradition in a form which was compatible to function as scripture for a generation which had not participated in the original events of revelation. The ordering of the tradition for this new function involved a profoundly hermeneutical activity, the effects of which are now built into the structure of the canonical text. For this reason an adequate interpretation of the biblical text, both in terms of history and theology, depends on taking the canonical shape with great seriousness. When seen in this light, the usual practice of the historical-critical Introduction of relegating a treatment of the canon to the final chapter is entirely misleading and deficient.

The Relation between the Literary and Canonical Histories

The recognition of the complex history of the growth of the Old Testament literature did more than anything else to bring about the collapse of the older dogmatic understanding of the canon. The formation of the Hebrew Bible could not be adequately handled without paying close attention to a history of literary development which shared many of the features of ancient Near Eastern literature in general. The implications of the discovery of this historical dimension in the literature's formation were soon drawn in respect to the canon as well. Obviously, the present form of the Hebrew canon was also a product of a historical development. But what is the relation between these two histories, namely, the history of the literature and the history of the canon?

The classic Wellhausen position of Old Testament criticism clearly recognized two distinct historical processes, but sought to relate them closely. Thus, the 'book of the law' discovered in 621 BC during the reign of Josiah was identified as the book of Deuteronomy, which was judged to be a seventh-century platform for the reforming party in Jerusalem. Its acceptance as an authority also marked the first stage of canonization of the Hexateuch according to the theory. As we have seen, the attack on Wellhausen's theory of the literary history of the Old Testament also fell on the reconstruction of the canonical history. In the recent search for a new reconstruction of the literary history of Israel there have been several attempts to identify the two processes, whether by means of a new literary-critical hypothesis (Freedman) or by a return to an older conservative position (Kline). In my judgment, this identification of the literary and the canonical history, whether stemming from the left or right of the theological spectrum, is a step backward and cannot be sustained.

The two processes are not to be identified, but clearly they belong together. Exactly how the two histories relate remains often unclear and much more intensive research will be needed to clarify the problem. Still a few general observations regarding their relationship are in order. First, the development of Hebrew literature involved a much broader history than the history of the canon's development. The former process resulted from innumerable forces such as laws of saga, the use of inherited literary patterns of prose and poetry, the social setting of diverse institutions, the changing scribal techniques etc., whereas the latter process was much more closely defined by those forces which affected the literature's evaluation, transmission, and usage. Although non-religious factors (political, social, and economic) certainly entered into the canonical process, these were subordinated to the religious usage of the literature by its function within the community.

Secondly, there were periods in the history of Israel in which the canonical history was largely subsumed under the history of the literature's development. This fusion of the two processes was especially evident during the early, pre-exilic history, but in the later exilic and post-exilic periods these forces associated with the development of canon increased in importance. There seems to be a direct relationship between the quantity of literature and the interest in its collection and ordering within set parameters.

Thirdly, because of the lack of historical evidence, it is extremely difficult to determine the motivations involved in the canonical process. The Old Testament neither reports directly on this history, nor does it even reflect a tradition of the canonical process. With the one exception of the Deuteronomic tradition of Moses' writing and preservation of the Book of the Law, the Old Testament has no tradition from which one could begin to recover its history. At most we find an occasional isolated event or situation from which some historical information can be inferred. For example, it remains exceedingly difficult to determine to what extent a canonical force was at work in the uniting of the J and E sources of the Pentateuch or how a consciousness of the canon exerted itself in the process.

Caution must be exercised not to hypothesize the history of the literature's growth in such a way as to eliminates *a priori* the religious dimensions associated with the function of the canon. One does not have to read far in the standard historical critical Introductions to find hypotheses regarding the literary and canonical histories which rest on untested historiographical assumptions.

A Sketch of the Development of the Hebrew Canon

The book of Deuteronomy (31.24ff.) records an act which clearly reflects an early stage in the growth of the canon. Moses wrote the words of the divine law in a book which was deposited by the side of the ark of the covenant for periodical reading before the entire assembly of Israel. Of course, the age of this chapter cannot be unequivocally fixed—many scholars would feel that it is pre-exilic—nor can the scope of the law attributed to Moses be determined with certainty. But from what we know of the history of the literature, it is not to be identified with the whole Pentateuch.

However, there is evidence to show that the Deuteronomic description of Moses' act stands in close continuity with earlier tradition. First, Moses' role as mediator of the divine law is deeply rooted in the Sinai tradition. When Israel was unable to receive the divine law directly, Moses interceded for the people. Moreover, Ex. 24.1–11, which belongs to the earliest strands of the Pentateuch, records Moses' writing the words of the law, reading them in an assembly of the people within a cultic context, and evoking a response of loyalty to their stipulations. But there is a difference between the two passages Deut. 31 and Ex. 24, which already indicates a growth in the history of canon. Both passages speak of an authoritative law written by Moses which was read in the hearing of the people. But in Deut. 31 the written form of the law has received a function far more autonomous than Ex. 24 in relation to its original historical setting. Deuteronomy 31.26 emphasizes the careful preservation of the book commensurate to its sacred quality. The words themselves, apart from Moses, function as an authoritative witness against rebellion. A set period in the future is prescribed for continual reading of the law whose authority is unimpaired by Moses' death.

The discovery of the book of the law in II Kings 22 (cf. II Chron. 34) did not mark the beginning of the canonical process, but provides a further historical confirmation of the already existing authority of the Mosaic law. Of course, many problems remain in establishing the history of the growth of the literature in the seventh century, which relate to the age, circle, and scope of the book of Deuteronomy, but in spite of these uncertainties, the passage does provide historical evidence for the canonical process.

There is further evidence in the canonical development of the Law of Moses to be found in the redactional framework which surrounds the Former Prophets. This sign of editorial activity is usually associated with a Deuteronomistic school in the sixth to fifth centuries. Thus, for example, in the book of Joshua the leadership of the nation is not conceived of as an extension of Moses' office, but is pictured as dependent upon the divine law revealed to Moses and preserved in book form (cf. 1.8; 4.10, etc.). Although the literary history of the late fifth century associated with the role of Ezra is not fully clear, most scholars would agree that the present form of the Pentateuch took its shape at this time. The legal prescriptions recorded in Neh. 8.13–18 reflect the Priestly code. Nevertheless, in terms of the history of the canon, the authority of the Mosaic law is further attested, but the exact extent of the canonical books comprising this law cannot be established from these texts. Nor does it seem possible from the evidence to understand in any detail the process by which the narrative material in the Pentateuch was accorded a similar canonical status to that of the laws.

Another type of evidence in tracing the history of the canon has been deduced from the development of the Hebrew text. Textual history of the Pentateuch can be reconstructed in some measure from the third century BC. One can easily project a history of textual development which had begun considerably earlier. This evidence would seem to confirm that the extent of a canonical corpus had already been settled by then and that the history of establishing the text of the sacred writings had begun. The translation of the Pentateuch into Greek from the middle of the third century is an indication of its authoritative status. The *terminus ad quem* of the canonization of the Pentateuch is provided at the beginning of the second century by Ben Sira whose knowledge and use of all the legal portions can only presuppose the canonical status of the entire Pentateuch (cf. Swanson, 88ff., *contra* Hölscher). Furthermore, there is nothing at Qumran to challenge this conclusion and much indirect evidence to support it.

Not surprisingly in the light of the paucity of evidence, scholarly opinions differ widely regarding the canonical history of the Prophets. The two extremes are marked, on the one hand, by Freedman and Leiman, who argue for a closing of the prophetic canon about 500–450 BC and Swanson, on the other hand, proposing an open collection of prophets well into the Christian era. The major evidence used in support of the first position is that the books themselves refer to no event after c. 500, that the Chronicler was too late to be included in this section, and that there was a tradition of the cessation of prophecy after Malachi. In my judgment, none of these arguments carry much historical weight, and they rest on assumptions which have already been criticized. The second position represented by Swanson argues that the designation 'Law and Prophets' included all scripture and that the tripartite division was a late, rabbinic development. In my opinion, Swanson's interpretation cannot be sustained without considerable modification. In spite of his argument, the repeated reference in the prologue of Ben Sira to 'the Law and the Prophets, and the remaining books' cannot be discounted. Moreover, that Ben Sira knows all the prophetic books in a canonical order (46.1–49.13) and even the title of the Book of the Twelve appears to be strong evidence for a fixed canonical unit of prophets by the beginning of the second century.

However, in spite of fixing a terminus to the history, the more important issues within the canonical process of the prophetic corpus remains still unresolved. There are a few early signs even from the pre-exilic period of a canon consciousness related to the prophetic preaching. In both Isa. 8.16 and Jer. 36.1ff. one sees the transition from the spoken prophetic word to a written form with authority. Later, there is reference in Zech. 1.4ff. to the 'former prophets' whose writings appear to have a form and authoritative status. The exegesis within the Bible itself in the post-exilic period begins to cite earlier oracles *verbatim* as an authoritative text which it seeks to interpret (cf. Isa. 65, 25, which echoes Isa. 1.6ff.). Finally, Dan. 9.2 offers evidence of some sort of fixed collection of prophetic writings.

The basic question of understanding the relation between the Law and the Prophets within the canonical history remains difficult to resolve. Although I do not regard Lebram's theory as correct which sees a series of authoritative prophetic writings preceding the canonical position of the Law, nevertheless, there are signs of mutual influence between the two developing collections. Since Moses was regarded as a prophet, his authority may well have extended to other books written by prophets. The close link between Deuteronomy and the Deuteronomistic editing of the Former Prophets would tend to confirm such an understanding. Certainly Clements (*Prophecy and Tradition*, 55) is right in emphasizing that the canonical process should not be conceived of as a closed section of Law to which the Prophets were joined only secondarily. At an early date the two collections, Law and Prophets, were joined and both experienced expansion. By the first century BC both sections of the canon were regarded as normative scripture (cf. Swanson, 178ff., on the Qumran evidence).

Again, evidence for tracing the canonical history of the final section of the Hebrew Bible, the Writings or Hagiographa, is sparse and highly contested. Sundberg has argued that the Jewish canon by the first century AD consisted of the Law and the Prophets as well as other religious writings which had not been established in a fixed collection. At the Council of Jamnia (c. AD 90) rabbinic Judaism narrowed its canon and excluded many of the religious writings which had been freely circulating up to that time. The forces behind this move have been variously explained as derived from an anti-apocalyptic or anti-Christian concern. From this loosely joined collection of excluded religious writings, the Christian church formed its larger canon.

Against this thesis, Leiman has protested that the extent of the Jewish canon had been settled long before AD 90. He has certainly made a strong case against making Jamnia a key stage in the history of the Jewish canon. The basic text (M. Yadayim 3.5) refers only to a discussion concerning the status of Ecclesiastes and Song of Songs, and not the other books of the Hagiographa. There is good reason to believe that the dispute was a scholastic enterprise (Talmon), turning on the inspired status of the books under consideration, and not canonicity. Moreover, there was no official ruling and debates continued on these same books long after Jamnia (cf. Leiman, *Canonization*, 120ff.).

Several other theories regarding the formation of the Hagiographa have been proposed. Swanson has even argued for the possibility that the bipartite collection of the Hebrew scriptures had been closed and the number of books restricted before the category known as the Writings was formed. In my judgment, Swanson's interpretation of Ben Sira, Josephus, and the New Testament, in which evidence for a tripartite division is usually found, has not been convincing. Still it is quite certain that other canonical arrangements were in competition during the second and first centuries and that the lines between the Prophets and the

Writings remained in considerable flux (cf. Katz). Clearly in the case of the book of Daniel, its canonical status was established independently of its location in one of the two canonical collections. Although conclusive evidence for dating the closing of the third section of the Jewish canon is not available, the stabilization of the Hebrew text by the end of the first century AD would further point to a relatively closed Hebrew canon by the beginning of the Christian era.

The problem of the so-called apocryphal books in relation to the Jewish canon has been much discussed in recent years (Sundberg, Leiman, Swanson). There is a consensus that during the Hellenistic period a much wider selection of religious writings were in use than those finally recognized as authoritative within the Jewish canon. Opinions vary on the authority accorded these books. The presence of many non-canonical writings at Qumran brought an additional confirmation to the wide scope of literature in use among Jews of this period. The canonization process within Judaism thus involved a selection of a limited number of books from a much larger resource of available literature. Moreover, this canonical limitation was not confined solely to Palestine, as Sundberg has shown.

The motivation lying behind this narrowing process has also been much debated. Usually, it has been attributed either to a growing conservatism within rabbinic Judaism, or to a fear of apocalyptic literature or to an anti-Christian move. Since the sources are virtually silent, these alleged motivation factors remain in the realm of hypothesis. From indirect evidence of later Jewish writings, the anti-Christian move seems the least likely of the theories. Nevertheless, the effect of the exclusion of the apocryphal and pseudepigraphical books can be clearly recognized in the subsequent history of Judaism. Pharisaic Judaism was increasingly set apart by the scope of its canon from other Jewish and Christian groups which continued to use non-canonical books with varying degrees of authority.

Summary and Implications

A brief summary of our conclusions from this history is in order. First of all, it should be incontrovertible that there was a genuine historical development involved in the formation of the canon and that any concept of canon which fails to reckon with this historical dimension is faulty. Secondly, the available historical evidence allows for only a bare skeleton of this development. One searches largely in vain for solid biblical or extra-biblical evidence by which to trace the real causes and motivations behind many of the crucial decisions. How did a writing exert an authority and on whom? What lay behind a particular collection of books at a given historical period? How were the variety of claims of authority related to one another and adjudicated? What groups were involved in the process and how were they affected by their historical milieu?

Certain methodological implications derive from these conclusions. We are faced with an obvious dilemma. Clearly the role of the canon is of fundamental importance in understanding the Hebrew scriptures. Yet the Jewish canon was formed through a complex historical process which is largely inaccessible to critical reconstruction. The history of the canonical process does not seem to be an avenue through which one can greatly illuminate the present canonical text. Not only is the evidence far too skeletal, but the sources seem to conceal the very kind of information which would allow a historian easy access into the material by means of uncovering the process. Is there any way out of this impasse?

CANON AND CRITICISM

Bibliography

N. **Appel**, *Kanon und Kirche*, Paderborn 1964; James **Barr**, 'Trends and Prospects in Biblical Theology', *JTS* NS 25, 1974, 265–82; 'Biblical Theology', *IDB Suppl*, 104–11; Karl **Barth**, *Church Dogmatics*, 1/1, ET New York 1936, Edinburgh 1938; 2nd ed. Edinburgh and Grand Rapids, Mich. 1975; *Die Schrift in der Kirche*, Zürich 1947; G. **Bornkamm**, 'Die ökumenische Bedeutung der historisch-kritischen Bibelwissenschaft', *Geschichte und Glaube* II, Munich 1971, 11–20; H. **Cazelles**, 'Biblical Criticism, OT', *IDB Suppl*, 98–102; B. S. **Childs**, 'The Old Testament as Scripture of the Church', *CTM* 43, 1972, 709–22; G. W. **Coats** and B. O. **Long**, eds., *Canon and Authority*, Philadelphia 1977; O. **Cullmann**, 'The Tradition', *The Early Church*, ET London and Philadelphia 1956; H. **Diem**, *Das Problem des Schriftkanons*, Zürich 1952; E. **Dobschütz**, 'The Abandonment of the Canonical Idea', *AJT* 19, 1915, 416ff.; P.-G. **Duncker**, 'The Canon of the Old Testament at the Council of Trent', *CBQ* 15, 1953, 277–99; G. **Ebeling**, 'The Significance of the Critical Historical Method for Church and Theology in Protestantism', *Word and Faith*, ET Philadelphia and London 1963, 17–61; '"Sola scriptura" und das Problem der Tradition', in *Das Neue Testament als Kanon*, ed. E. Käsemann (see below), 282–335; O. C. **Edwards** Jr., 'Historical Critical Method's Failure of Nerve and a Prescription for a Tonic', *AThR* 59, 1977, 115–34; C. F. **Evans**, *Is Holy Scripture Christian?*, London 1971. F. V. **Filson**, *Which Books Belong in the Bible? A Study of the Canon*, Philadelphia 1957; I. **Frank**, *Der Sinn Der Kanonbildung*, Freiburg 1971; J. **Gerhard**, *Loci Theologici*, Tübingen 1762, Tom. I, Locus I, chs. I–II, 1–13; H. **Gese**, 'Erwägung zur Einheit der biblischen Theologie', *ZTK* 67, 1970, 417–36, reprinted in *Vom Sinai zum Zion*, Munich 1974, 11–30; B. **Hägglund**, 'Die Bedeutung der "regula fidei" als Grundlage theologischer Aussagen', *StTh* 11, 1957, 1–44; F. **Hahn**, 'Das Problem "Schrift und Tradition" im Urchristentum', *EvTh* 39, 1970, 449–68; H. H. **Howorth**, 'The Origin and Authority of the Biblical Canon according to the Continental Reformers', *JTS* 8, 1906–7, 321–65; 'The Origin and Authority of the Canon among the Later Reformers', *JTS* 10, 1908–9, 183–232; 'The Influence of St Jerome on the Canon of the Western Church, II', *JTS* 11, 1909–10, 321–47; M. **Jugie**, *Histoire du canon de l'Ancien Testament dans l'église grecque et l'église russe*, Paris 1909, reprinted Leipzig 1974; E. **Käsemann**, 'Vom theologischen

Recht historisch-kritischer Exegese', *ZTK* 64, 1967, 259–81; ed., *Das Neue Testament als Kanon*, Göttingen 1970; D. H. **Kelsey**, *The Uses of Scripture in Recent Theology*, Philadelphia and London 1975; H.-J. **Kraus**, 'Zur Geschichte des Überlieferungsbegriffs in der alttestament-lichen Wissenschaft', *EvTh* 16, 1956, 371–87, reprinted in *Biblisch-theologische Aufsätze*, Neukirchen-Vluyn 1972, 278–95; E. **Krentz**, *The Historical Critical Method*, Philadelphia 1975; H. **Küng**, 'Der Frühkatholizismus im Neuen Testament also kontroverstheologisches Problem', in *Das Neue Testament als Kanon*, ed. E. Käsemann, 175–204. M.-J. **Lagrange**, *La méthode historique*, Paris 1966; A. N. E. **Lane**, 'Scripture, Tradition and Church: An Historical Survey', *Vox Evangelica* 9, London 1975, 37–55; P. **Lengsfeld**, *Überlieferung. Tradition und Schrift in der evangelischen und katholischen Theologie der Gegenwart*, Paderborn 1960; I. **Lönning**, '*Kanon im Kanon*', Oslo 1972; A. **Maichle**, *Der Kanon der biblischen Bücher und das Konzil von Trent*, Freiburg 1929; G. **Maier**, *Das Ende des historisch-kritischen Methode*, Wuppertal 1974; F. **Mildenberger**, *Gottes Tat im Wort*, Gütersloh 1964; *Die halbe Wahrheit oder die ganze Bibel*, Munich 1967; J. H. **Newman**, 'On the Interpretation of Scripture', *The Nineteenth Century* 15, London 1884, 185–99; D. E. **Nineham**, *The Use and Abuse of the Bible*, London 1976; S. M. **Ogden**, 'The Authority of Scripture for Theology', *Interp* 30, 1976, 242–70; K.-H. **Ohlig**, *Woher nimmt die Bibel ihre Autorität? Zum Verhältnis von Schriftkanon, Kirche und Jesus*, Düsseldorf 1970; *Die theologische Begründung des neutestamentlichen Kanons in der alten Kirche*, Düsseldorf 1972; Eva **Osswald**, 'Zum Problem der hermeneutischen Relevanz des Kanons für die Interpretation alttestamentlicher Texte', *Theologische Versuche* 18, East Berlin 1978; F. **Overbeck**, *Zur Geschichte des Kanons*, 1880, reprinted Darmstadt 1965; P. **Ricoeur**, *La métaphore vive*, Paris 1975; *Conflict of Interpretation*, ET Evanston 1976; J. F. A. **Sawyer**, 'The "Original Meaning of the Text," and Other Legitimate Subjects for Semantic Description', *BETL* 33, 1974, 63–70; E. **Schlink**, 'Zum Problem der Tradition', *Der kommende Christus und die kirchlichen Tradition*, Göttingen 1961, 196–201; W. **Schrage**, 'Die Frage nach der Mitte und dem Kanon im Kanon des Neuen Testaments in der neueren Diskussion', *Rechtfertigung, FS E. Käsemann*, Tübingen 1976, 415–42; S. J. **Schultz**, 'Augustine and the Old Testament Canon', *Bibliotheca Sacra* 113, Dallas 1955, 225–34; E. **Schweizer**, 'Kanon?', *EvTh* 31, 1971, 339–57. G. T. **Sheppard**, 'Canon Criticism: The Proposal . . . and an Assessment for Evangelical Hermeneutics', *Studia Biblica et Theologica* 4, Pasadena, Calif. 1974, 3–17; R. **Smend**, 'Nachkritische Schriftauslegung', *Parresia, FS Karl Barth*, Zürich 1966, 215–37; W. **Staerk**, 'Der Schrift- und Kanonbegriff der jüdischen

Bibel', *Zeitschrift für systematische Theologie* 6, Berlin 1929, 101–19;
P. **Stuhlmacher**, 'Historische Kritik und theologische Schriftauslegung',
Schriftauslegung auf dem Wege zur biblischen Theologies, Göttingen 1975,
59–127; G. H. **Tavard**, *Holy Writ or Holy Church*, London 1959, New
York 1960; E. **Troeltsch**, 'Über historische und dogmatische Methode
in der Theologie', reprinted *Theologie als Wissenschaft*, ed. G. Sauter,
ThB 43, 1971, 105–27; B. B. **Warfield**, 'Inspiration and Criticism', *The
Inspiration and Authority of the Bible*, Philadelphia 1948, London 1951,
419–42; W. **Wink**, *The Bible in Human Transformations*, Philadelphia 1973;
H. W. **Wolff**, 'Zur Hermeneutik des Alten Testaments', 1956, reprinted
GSAT, Munich 1964, 251–88; G. E. **Wright**, *The Old Testament and
Theology*, New York 1969.

The purpose of this chapter is to describe an approach within the
discipline of Old Testament Introduction which will attempt to
overcome the methodological impasse of the canon which has been
described in the previous chapter. Its goal is to take seriously the
significance of the canon as a crucial element in understanding
the Hebrew scriptures, and yet to understand the canon in its true
historical and theological dimensions. It will seek to relate the
canonical form of the Old Testament to the complex history of
the literature's formation, the discovery of which is the hallmark
of the modern historical critical study of the Bible.

Throughout this Introduction I shall be criticizing the failure of
the historical critical method, as usually practised, to deal adequately with the canonical literature of the Old Testament. Nevertheless, it is a basic misunderstanding of the canonical approach to
describe it as a non-historical reading of the Bible. Nothing could
be further from the truth! Rather, the issue at stake is the nature
of the Bible's historicity and the search for a historical approach
which is commensurate with it. The whole point of emphasizing
the canon is to stress the historical nature of the biblical witness.
There is no 'revelation' apart from the experience of historical Israel.
However, a general hermeneutic is inadequate to deal with the particular medium through which this experience has been registered.

The study of the canonical shape of the literature is an attempt to do justice to the nature of Israel's unique history. To take the canon seriously is to stress the special quality of the Old Testament's humanity which is reflected in the form of Israel's sacred scripture.

Exegesis in a Canonical Context

At the outset I should like to set certain parameters to the scope of this study. The larger problems for Christian theology of establishing the relation between the two Testaments, as well as of examining the claims of the apocryphal books on the Christian church, lie beyond the scope of this Introduction to the Hebrew scriptures. In my judgment, these important subjects belong to the fields of biblical theology, New Testament, and early church history. However, I will at least express my own conviction regarding the importance of the study of the Hebrew scriptures for Christian theology. It is insufficient that the Christian church seeks to relate itself in some way with the historical events of the Old Testament. Rather, it is essential for a theological relationship to be maintained between the people of the Old Covenant and of the New. Regardless of whatever other writings or traditions were deemed authoritative by each community within a larger canon—for Jews it is the tradition of the sages, for Christians the gospel of Jesus Christ—the common canon of the Hebrew scriptures provides the fundamental basis for any serious relationship. I am well aware that this is a prescriptive statement, and that only seldom has either of the two communities of faith functioned in a way which reflected the common canon of sacred scripture. To seek to trace the development of the Christian canon within the church and to do justice to both the historical and theological problems involved far exceeds the scope of this present enterprise. For this reason the discussion which follows will limit itself, by and large, to the Hebrew scriptures. Only in the final chapter will I return to a reflection on these broader issues of Biblical Theology.

The major task of a canonical analysis of the Hebrew Bible is a descriptive one. It seeks to understand the peculiar shape and special function of these texts which comprise the Hebrew canon. Such an analysis does not assume a particular stance or faith commitment on the part of the reader because the subject of the investigation is the literature of Israel's faith, not that of the reader. However, apart from unintentional bias which is always present to some extent, the religious stance of the modern reader can play a legitimate role after the descriptive task has been accomplished, when the reader chooses whether or not to identify with the perspectives of the canonical texts of Israel which he has studied. Because this literature has had a special history as the religious literature of ancient Israel, its peculiar features must be handled in a way compatible to the material itself. A corpus of religious writings which has been transmitted within a community for over a thousand years cannot properly be compared to inert shreds which have lain in the ground for centuries. This observation is especially in order when one recognizes that Israel's developing religious understanding—the Bible speaks of God's encounter with Israel—left its mark on the literature in a continuing process of reshaping and growth.

Canonical analysis focuses its attention on the final form of the text itself. It seeks neither to use the text merely as a source for other information obtained by means of an oblique reading, nor to reconstruct a history of religious development. Rather, it treats the literature in its own integrity. Its concern is not to establish a history of Hebrew literature in general, but to study the features of this peculiar set of religious texts in relation to their usage within the historical community of ancient Israel. To take the canonical shape of these texts seriously is to seek to do justice to a literature which Israel transmitted as a record of God's revelation to his people along with Israel's response. The canonical approach to the Hebrew Bible does not make any dogmatic claims for the literature apart from the literature itself, as if these texts contained only timeless truths or communicated in a unique idiom, but rather it studies them as historically and theologically conditioned writings which were accorded a normative function in the life of this community. It also acknowledges that the texts served a religious function in closest relationship to the worship and service of God whom Israel confessed to be the source of the sacred word. The witness of the text cannot be separated from the divine reality which Israel testified to have evoked the response.

It is a misunderstanding of the canonical method to characterize it as an attempt to bring extrinsic, dogmatic categories to bear on the biblical text by which to stifle the genuine exegetical endeavour. Rather, the approach seeks to work within that interpretative structure which the biblical text has received from those who formed and used it as sacred scripture. To understand that canonical shape requires the highest degree of exegetical skill in an intensive wrestling with the text. It is to be expected that interpreters will sometimes disagree on the nature of the canonical shaping, but the disagreement will enhance the enterprise if the various interpreters share a common understanding of the nature of the exegetical task.

The Canonical Approach Contrasted with Others

Several crucial methodological issues are raised when the canonical approach is described as focusing on the final form of the text. Perhaps these issues can be most sharply profiled by contrasting the approach which I am suggesting with other familiar methods of critical biblical scholarship.

The canonical study of the Old Testament shares an interest in common with several of the newer literary critical methods in its concern to do justice to the integrity of the text itself apart from diachronistic reconstruction. One thinks of the so-called newer criticism of English studies, of various forms of structural analysis, and of rhetorical criticism. Yet the canonical approach differs from a strictly literary approach by interpreting the biblical text in relation to a community of faith and practice for whom it served a particular theological role as possessing divine authority. For theological reasons the biblical texts were often shaped in such a way that the original poetic forms were lost, or a unified narrative badly shattered. The canonical approach is concerned to understand the nature of the theological shape of the text rather than to recover an original literary or aesthetic unity. Moreover, it does not agree with a form of structuralism which seeks to reach a depth structure of meaning lying below the surface of the canonical text.

Then again, the canonical method which is being outlined differs sharply from the so-called kerygmatic exegesis which was popularized by von Rad and his students in the '50s and '60s. Classic examples of this method can be found in the writings of H. W. Wolff, C. Westermann, W. Brueggemann, among others. For several years beginning in 1966 *Interpretation* ran a series of articles under the rubric '*Kerygma* of the Bible'. This method attempted to discover the central intention of a writer, usually by means of formulae or themes, which intention was then linked to a reconstruction of a historical situation which allegedly evoked that given response. Its major concern was to combine historical critical analysis with a type of theological interpretation. A major criticism of the method is the extremely subjective, reductionist method in which the form-critical method has been extended beyond its original function to derive a theological message. Often the assumption that the theological point must be related to an original intention within a reconstructed historical context runs directly in the face of the literature's explicit statement of its function within the final form of the biblical text. The fragile nature of this kind of exegesis is also illustrated by its heavy dependence upon critical theories which bear less and less weight (von Rad's Credo, Noth's amphictyony, etc.).

Again, the canonical study of the Old Testament is to be distinguished from the traditio-critical approach in the way in which it evaluates the history of the text's formation. By assuming the normative status of the final form of the text the canonical approach evokes the strongest opposition from the side of traditio-historical criticism for which the heart of the exegetical task is the recovery of the depth dimension. Form critics raise familiar questions: Why should one stage in the process be accorded a special status? Were not the earlier levels of the text once regarded as canonical as well, and why should they not continue to be so regarded within the exegetical enterprise? Is not the history which one recovers in the growth of a text an important index for studying Israel's development of a self-understanding, and thus the very object of Old Testament theology? Having been trained in the form-critical method, I feel the force of these questions and am aware of the value of the approach. Still I feel strongly that these questions miss the mark and have not fully grasped the methodological issues at stake in the canonical proposal.

The Final Form of the Text and Its Prehistory

The reason for insisting on the final form of scripture lies in the peculiar relationship between text and people of God which is constitutive of the canon. The shape of the biblical text reflects a history of encounter between God and Israel. The canon serves to describe this peculiar relationship and to define the scope of this history by establishing a beginning and end to the process. It assigns a special quality to this particular segment of human history which became normative for all successive generations of this community of faith. The significance of the final form of the biblical text is that it alone bears witness to the full history of revelation. Within the Old Testament neither the process of the formation of the literature nor the history of its canonization is assigned an independent integrity. This dimension has often been lost or purposely blurred and is therefore dependent on scholarly reconstruction. The fixing of a canon of scripture implies that the witness to Israel's experience with God lies not in recovering such historical processes, but is testified to in the effect on the biblical text itself. Scripture bears witness to God's activity in history on Israel's behalf, but history *per se* is not a medium of revelation which is commensurate with a canon. It is only in the final form of the biblical text in which the normative history has reached an end that the full effect of this revelatory history can be perceived.

It is certainly true that earlier stages in the development of the biblical literature were often regarded as canonical prior to the establishment of the final form. In fact, the final form frequently consists of simply transmitting an earlier, received form of the tradition often unchanged from its original setting. Yet to take the canon seriously is also to take seriously the critical function which it exercises in respect to the earlier stages of the literature's formation. A critical judgment is evidenced in the way in which these earlier stages are handled. At times the material is passed on unchanged; at other times tradents select, rearrange, or expand the received tradition. The purpose of insisting on the authority of the final canonical form is to defend its role of providing this critical norm. To work with the final stage of the text is not to lose the historical dimension, but rather to make a critical, theological judgment regarding the process. The depth dimension aids in understanding the interpreted text, and does not function independently of it. To distinguish the Yahwist source from the Priestly in the Pentateuch often allows the interpreter to hear the combined texts with new precision. But it is the full, combined text which has rendered a judgment on the shape of the tradition and which continues to exercise an authority on the community of faith. Of course, it is legitimate and fully necessary for the historian of the ancient Near East to use his written evidence in a different manner, often reading his texts obliquely, but this enterprise is of a different order from the interpretation of sacred scripture which we are seeking to describe.

Then again, the final form of the text performs a crucial hermeneutical function in establishing the peculiar profile of a passage. Its shaping provides an order in highlighting certain elements and subordinating others, in drawing features to the foreground and pushing others into the background. To work from the final form is to resist any method which seeks critically to shift the canonical ordering. Such an exegetical move occurs whenever an overarching category such as *Heilsgeschichte* subordinates the peculiar canonical profile, or a historical critical reconstruction attempts to refocus the picture according to its own standards of aesthetics or historical accuracy.

Although much of my polemical attention up to now has been directed against various forms of historicism which have made the use of the Bible dependent upon a reconstructed form of historical events rather than on the final form of the canonical text, I am also aware that another, very different front has been opened up which is equally incompatible with the canonical approach. In the philosophical hermeneutics of Paul Ricoeur and his followers the Bible is seen as a deposit of metaphors which contains inherent powers by which to interpret and order the present world of experience, regardless of the source of the imagery. The concern is to illuminate what lies 'ahead' (*devant*) of the text, not behind. This approach shows little or no interest in the historical development of the biblical text or even in the historical context of the canonical text. The crucial interpretative context in which the metaphors function is provided by the faith community itself (cf. D. Kelsey). Such an approach fails to take seriously the essential function of the canon in grounding the biblical metaphors within the context of historic Israel. By shaping Israel's traditions into the form of a normative scripture the biblical idiom no longer functions for the community of faith as free-floating metaphor, but as the divine imperative and promise to a historically conditioned people of God whose legacy the Christian church confesses to share.

The Canonical Process and the Shaping of Scripture

The formation of the canon took place over an extended period of time in close relation to the development of the Hebrew literature. But the canonical process was not simply an external validation of successive stages of literary development, but was an integral part of the literary process. Beginning in the pre-exilic period, but increasing in significance in the post-exilic era, a force was unleashed by Israel's religious use of her traditions which exerted an influence on the shaping of the literature as it was selected, collected, and ordered. It is clear from the sketch of the process that particular editors, religious groups, and even political parties were involved. At times one can describe these groups historically or sociologically, such as the reforming Deuteronomic party of Jerusalem, or the editors associated with Hezekiah's court (Prov. 25.1). But basic to the canonical process is that those responsible for the actual editing of the text did their best to obscure their own identity. Thus the actual process by which the text was reworked lies in almost total obscurity. Its presence is detected by the effect on the text. Moreover, increasingly the original sociological and historical differences within the nation of Israel—Northern and Southern Kingdom, pro- and anti-monarchial parties, apocalyptic versus theocratic circles— were lost, and a religious community emerged which found its identity in terms of sacred scripture. Israel defined itself in terms of a book! The canon formed the decisive *Sitz im Leben* for the Jewish community's life, thus blurring the sociological evidence most sought after by the modern historian. When critical exegesis is made to rest on the recovery of these very sociological distinctions which have been obscured, it runs directly in the face of the canon's intention.

The motivations behind the canonical process were diverse and seldom discussed in the biblical text itself. However, the one concern which is expressly mentioned is that a tradition from the past be transmitted in such a way that its authoritative claims be laid upon all successive generations of Israel. Such expressions of intent are found in the promulgation of the law (Deut. 31.9ff.), in the fixing of rituals (Ex. 12.14), and in the provisions for transmitting the sacred story (Ex. 12.26ff.). A study of the biblical text reveals that this concern to pass on the authoritative tradition did not consist in merely passively channelling material from one generation to another, but reflects an involvement which actively shaped both the oral and written traditions. A major hermeneutical move was effected in the process of forming an original law, prophetic oracles, or ancient narrative into a collection of scripture through which every subsequent generation was to be addressed.

It is not clear to what extent the ordering of the oral and written material into a canonical form always involved an intentional decision. At times there is clear evidence for an intentional blurring of the original historical setting (cf. the discussion of 'Second Isaiah'). At other times the canonical shaping depends largely on what appear to be unintentional factors which subsequently were incorporated within a canonical context (e.g. the sequence of the proverbs in Prov. 10ff.). But irrespective of intentionality the effect of the canonical process was to render the tradition accessible to the future generation by means of a 'canonical intentionality', which is coextensive with the meaning of the biblical text.

The implication of this understanding of canon is crucial for one's approach to the problem of the 'actualization' of the biblical text. In the recent hermeneutical debate the term actualization (*Vergegenwärtigung*) denoted that process by which an ancient historical text was rendered accessible to a modern religious usage.

An axiom of much redactional criticism is that the layering of a biblical text derives chiefly from a need to 'update' an original tradition. Although this description occasionally applies (Isa. 16.13f.), the chief point to be made by the canonical approach is that actualization is by no means limited to this one model. Rather, it is constitutive of the canon to seek to transmit the tradition in such a way as to prevent its being moored in the past. Actualization derives from a hermeneutical concern which was present during the different stages of the book's canonization. It is built into the structure of the text itself, and reveals an enormous richness of theological interpretation by which to render the text religiously accessible. The modern hermeneutical impasse which has found itself unable successfully to bridge the gap between the past and the present has arisen in large measure from its disregard of the canonical shaping. The usual critical method of biblical exegesis is, first, to seek to restore an original historical setting by stripping away those very elements which constitute the canonical shape. Little wonder that once the biblical text has been securely anchored in the historical past by 'decanonizing' it, the interpreter has difficulty applying it to the modern religious context. (I am indebted to Gerald T. Sheppard for this formulation of the issue.)

Scripture and Tradition

One of the most difficult theological problems of the canonical approach to the Old Testament involves understanding the relationship between the divine initiative in creating Israel's scripture and the human response in receiving and transmitting the authoritative Word. Christian theology has, by and large, continued to describe the Bible in traditional terminology as the 'Word of God' which implies divine authorship in some sense. Nevertheless, few theologians in this post-critical era would wish to deny that the active human participation in the hearing, writing, and transmission of the Bible is an absolutely necessary feature for correctly under-standing the text. What then is the relationship between these two dimensions of the Bible?

It is impossible to discuss the problem without being aware of the long and heated controversy within Christian theology which has strongly affected the history of exegesis, and has usually been treated under the rubric of 'Scripture and Tradition'. In the sixteenth century a sharp polarity developed between Protestant insistence on the primacy of the Bible and the Roman Catholic claim of ecclesiasti-cal authority. The Reformers argued that the Bible was authoritative, not because the church made it so, but because of the Word of God which it contained. The Roman Catholic theologians countered that the church had been the human medium through which the Spirit of God had given the scriptures a concrete form and thus tradition could not be set in subordination to Word.

This polemical impasse continued to play an important role throughout the seventeenth century and provided the framework in which much of the historical critical research first emerged (cf. Simon, Le Clerc, Carpzov, etc.). By the middle of the nineteenth century the widespread recognition of the historical dimension in the formation of the Bible had badly damaged the traditional dog-matic positions of both Protestants and Catholics. The older theo-logical issue was lost in the new historical and literary concerns to understand the growth of the literature. Within the dominant crit-ical circles of Liberal Protestantism the role of God in the Bible's formation was relegated to a loosely defined divine purpose lying somewhere behind the evolution of Israel's religion.

The rebirth of confessional theology within Protestantism following World War I brought a renewed emphasis on the pri-macy of the Word of God, roughly analogous to the position of the sixteenth-century Reformers. However, there was a major dif-ference in the attempt to accommodate orthodox Christian theol-ogy to the nineteenth-century historical critical study of the Bible.

Several different models were suggested which sought to maintain the full divine initiative, but also to accord theological integrity to the historical process in the formation of the scriptures. Within Roman Catholic theology several important theological developments also occurred in this same period, reflected in the papal encyclical of 1943, *Divino afflante spiritu*, and culminating in the theological formulations of Vatican II. First, there was an attempt to offer a more positive view of the results of the historical critical method, which up to that time had been largely negative as a reaction to the earlier Modernist threat. Secondly, in terms of the scripture and tradition problem the new Catholic formulation re-emphasized the active role of the church in the Bible's formation but in a way which did not jeopardize the primacy of the divine Word. Only occasionally was the older Roman position defended. In sum, there has been a remarkable theological rapprochement between Protestants and Catholics regarding the traditional controversy over scripture and tradition. Both camps have returned to a position more akin to that of the early church in which the two elements were closely related, but not fused, in a rule of faith. It is also significant to observe that both the threat and promise arising from the challenge of the historical critical method exerted an important factor in this theological reconciliation.

The major purpose of this brief historical review is to suggest that the canonical method is not tied to one narrowly conceived dogmatic stance respecting the problem of scripture and tradition. The approach seeks to work descriptively within a broad theological framework and is open to a variety of different theological formulations which remains the responsibility of the systematic theologian to develop. I would admit, however, that the canonical method which is here described does run counter to two extreme theological positions. It is incompatible with a position on the far right which would stress the divine initiative in such a way as to rule out any theological significance to the response to the divine Word by the people of God. It is equally incompatible with a position on the far theological left, which would understand the formation of the Bible in purely humanistic terms, such as Israel's search for self-identity, or a process within nature under which God is subsumed.

It is also my sincere hope that Jewish scholars will not feel excluded from the theological enterprise associated with the canon. Even though the language used in the debate tends to stem from Christian circles, the theological issue of Israel's role in the canonical process lies at the heart of Jewish tradition. In my judgment, much of the failure of the usual Jewish-Christian dialogue to achieve a serious theological dimension arises from the loss of a sense of a common Bible which is precisely the issue addressed by the canon.

At the conclusion of each chapter of the descriptive analysis of the Old Testament books, I have added a brief bibliography of the history of exegesis including both Jewish and Christian contributions. Attention to the subsequent history of interpretation of the Bible is absolutely essential for its understanding, but the topic is so immense as to exceed the boundaries suitable for an Introduction. Obviously the purpose of pursuing this history is not to suggest that biblical scholarship needs only to return to the past, but that the future task is sorely impoverished if the great insights of our predecessors are overlooked. Particularly in the search for the canonical shape of a biblical book, pre-critical interpreters often saw dimensions of the text more clearly than those whose perspective was brought into focus by purely historical questions. Conversely, the history of exegesis illustrates some perennial, even ontological, errors in mishearing the text which continue to find new support.

Canon and Interpretation

A final word is in order regarding the effect of the canon on the larger exegetical enterprise of interpreting the Old Testament.

The approach which I am undertaking has been described by others as 'canonical criticism'. I am unhappy with this term because it implies that the canonical approach is considered another historical critical technique which can take its place alongside of source criticism, form criticism, rhetorical criticism, and similar methods. I do not envision the approach to canon in this light. Rather, the issue at stake in relation to the canon turns on establishing a stance from which the Bible can be read as sacred scripture.

The concern with canon plays both a negative and a positive role in delineating the scope of exegesis. On the one hand, its negative role consists in relativizing the claims to priority of the historical critical method. It strongly resists the assumption that every biblical text has first to be filtered through a set historical critical mesh before one can even start the task of interpretation. On the other hand, its positive role seeks to challenge the interpreter to look closely at the biblical text in its received form and then critically to discern its function for a community of faith. Attention to the canon establishes certain parameters within which the tradition was placed. The canonical shaping serves not so much to establish a given meaning to a particular passage as to chart the boundaries within which the exegetical task is to be carried out.

Attention to these canonical guidelines within this Introduction may seem overly formalistic and too frequently concerned with determining a book's structure or interpretative patterns. However, one should not confuse this one aspect of the canonical approach with the full range of responsibilities comprising the exegetical task. A canonical Introduction is not the end, but only the beginning of exegesis. It prepares the stage for the real performance by clearing away unnecessary distractions and directing one's attention to the main activity which is about to be initiated.

In one sense the canonical method sets limits on the exegetical task by taking seriously the traditional parameters. In another sense the method liberates from the stifling effect of academic scholasticism. By insisting on viewing the exegetical task as constructive as well as descriptive, the interpreter is forced to confront the authoritative text of scripture in a continuing theological reflection. By placing the canonical text within the context of the community of faith and practice a variety of different exegetical models are freed to engage the text, such as the liturgical or the dramatic. In sum, the canon establishes a platform from which exegesis is launched rather than a barrier by which creative activity is restrained.

Theology as Testimony

Walter Brueggemann

INTERPRETATION IN A PLURALISTIC CONTEXT

It remains to consider what may come next in Old Testament theology, to anticipate where theological interpretation of the Old Testament may next turn and what shapes it may take. I cannot prognosticate with any certainty, or with much confidence, but I offer some comments that are complementary to the retrospect that I offered in chapters 1 and 2.

Disestablishment: From Hegemonic Interpretation to Pluralism

The great fact of the emerging context of theological interpretation of the Old Testament is *the disestablishment of our usual modes of interpretation and the parallel disestablishment of the institutional vehicles of such interpretation.* That is, disestablishment concerns both epistemological and sociopolitical factors, for as Karl Marx understood most clearly, knowledge and power are intimately connected ("the ideas of the dominant class become the dominant ideas"). This disestablishment is an exceedingly important matter for Old Testament theology, even though the establishment assumptions of long-established scholarship were not particularly noticed, critiqued, or valued; for to be established entails not noticing that one is established, and not entertaining the thought that it could be otherwise.

The establishment assumptions that have long dominated Old Testament theological interpretation have been of two kinds. On the one hand, Old Testament theology, as a Christian enterprise, could assume that it was dealing with the normative socio-religious-moral convictions of the West. It could therefore readily entertain a direct flow to the New Testament, because the dominant West was a Christian West. It could, moreover, assume that it studied the text that was generally taken as the normative text of the West, which carried with it more or less normative interpretations.[1]

On the other hand, Old Testament theology, in its centrist forms, has been largely an academic matter, shaped in German universities, slightly altered in the great graduate schools of the United States, and taught in United States theological seminaries by those educated in the university tradition. This academic shaping assured that Old Testament theology—in its epistemological assumptions, which are still very powerful—from the eighteenth century on would be an Enlightenment enterprise, in which the Cartesian skeptic and the Kantian knower would prevail over the text. These epistemological assumptions, by the nineteenth century,

---

1 On this function and character of the biblical text, see Northrop Frye, *The Great Code: The Bible and Literature* (London: Routledge and Kegan Paul, 1982).

were committed to (a) historicism that could determine "what happened," for there could be no meaning beyond "what happened"; (b) evolutionism, so that religious development occurred in a straight line of unilateral progress from the primitive to the sophisticated; and (c) a rationalism that felt a need to explain away much of the contradiction that violated "reasonableness" or that made claims beyond a naturalistic, scientifically available world.

Established modes of scholarship consisted in a rather uneasy but widely shared settlement that theological claims of an idealistic and triumphal kind could be sustained in the midst of critical scrutiny, a compromise that is perhaps inevitable in a modern world where Enlightenment modes of knowledge had declared war on theological tradition, but where the Bible as the subject of scholarship would not fully yield to such modes of knowledge, nor would the institutions of interpretation fully yield to a purely skeptical approach, the university no more than the church.[2]

My purpose here is not to attack or malign this phase of scholarship, for as far as Old Testament interpretation was concerned, there was nothing sinister about this enterprise.[3] Rather it is my

---

2 We may cite G. Ernest Wright as a model figure in the United States who embraced and practiced this uneasy, widely shared settlement with great effectiveness. He was a vigorous critical historian, yet managed to turn his research toward theological affirmation. On this uneasy settlement in U.S. scholarship, see Leo G. Perdue, *The Collapse of History: Reconstructing Old Testament Theology* (OBT; Minneapolis: Fortress Press, 1994) 19–44.

3 More recently, criticism that kept a check on more programmatic skepticism has given way, in some quarters, to criticism that is militantly and admittedly skeptical. Thus in his recent study, David Penchansky, *The Politics of Biblical Theology: A Postmodern Reading* (StABH 10; Macon, Ga.: Mercer University Press, 1995) 5, can speak of younger scholars who have "hatred" toward the older perspectives that operated with theological assumptions. The source and power of this hatred are yet to be explored, but they likely have to do with a great deal beyond academic, critical questions.

judgment that Old Testament interpretation, and theological interpretation more generally, cannot escape the epistemological and
political context in which it operates, and our forebears could do so
no more than we can. It is relatively easy to critique that enterprise.[4]
But that is not my purpose, for everything we are now able to do is
dependent on that era of study. My purpose is rather to recognize
that it was, like all serious interpretation, intensely context-bound,
in this case bound to the context of positivistic historicism.[5]

This alliance between triumphalist Christendom and critical
positivism produced a pattern of hegemonic interpretation.[6] How
could it do otherwise? It is this hegemonic pattern of interpretation
that now needs to be noticed, and that now is in enormous jeopardy. The hegemony assumed Christian-normative truth as taught
by the church, hedged about and kept intellectually respectable by
criticism that was also hegemonic—that is, a centrist project built
on consensus assumptions. This hegemonic practice meant that,
give or take some adjustments, there was a central, consensus
practice, and the fact that it was undertaken almost exclusively by
white, Western males is both a cause and a consequence of its dominance. Moreover, there was a monopoly of interpretation: only a
few did it with any visible influence or effect, and everyone knew

---

4 See the generous but critical assessment of Perdue, *The Collapse of
   History*, and the more aggressive dismissal of that enterprise by Penchansky, *The Politics of Biblical Theology*. The difference between the
   perspectives of Perdue and Penchansky in tone and outlook is worth
   noting. In my judgment, Perdue takes into account the context of
   that older scholarship, a matter that seems to interest Penchansky very
   little.

5 See Perdue, *The Collapse of History*, 3–68.

6 Jon Levenson, *The Hebrew Bible, the Old Testament, and Historical Criticism: Jews and Christians in Biblical Studies* (Louisville: Westminster/
   John Knox, 1993), especially chaps. 4–5, makes a vigorous critique of
   both Christian appropriation of the Hebrew Bible and the numbing
   effect of positivistic criticism.

who they were. This social establishment, like every social establishment, maintained itself by limiting access and membership
through the alliance of church authority and academic criteria. I
imagine that this hegemonic enterprise was sustained as long as it
was because the world it produced "worked," and dissidents could
be easily contained or silenced. One begins to notice the "masters
of suspicion" in the period of positivistic historicism, but only now
have dissidence and variation become so deep and so broad as to
challenge the hegemony in serious and effective ways.[7]

The disestablishment of a triumphalist church in the West
can hardly be contested. In the place of a consensus authority, we
have within the church an amazing pluralism that is matched outside the church by vigorous, competing religious claims and by a
profound secularization of culture. It is especially evident that the
Enlightenment establishment with which the church in its dominance had allied itself is equally disestablished.[8] As a consequence,
even within the university, confidence in positivistic rationality is
much challenged, in the sciences as in the humanities. What goes
under the general term of *postmodern* signifies the breakup of any

---

7   The notion of "masters of suspicion" is provided by Paul Ricoeur,
    Freud and Philosophy: An Essay in Interpretation (New Haven: Yale
    University Press, 1970) 32–36 and passim, as he makes reference to
    Freud, Marx, and Nietzsche.

8   It was perhaps the events surrounding the Watergate scandal and the
    Vietnam War that lethally damaged the legitimacy of Enlightenment
    institutions. Anyone who remembers the Vietnam War with any
    critical sensitivity will recall the arrogance of Henry Kissinger and
    McGeorge Bundy, major university figures, in claiming their monop-
    oly of knowledge about the war. See David Halberstam, *The Best and
    the Brightest* (New York: Fawcett Books, 1992); and see the belated,
    sad acknowledgments of Robert S. McNamara and Brian Vandemark,
    In Retrospect: The Tragedy and Lessons of Vietnam (New York: Random
    House, 1995). The crisis of confidence around these events can hardly
    be overestimated in its importance for the new U.S. context in which
    biblical interpretation must now be done.

broad consensus about what we know or how we know what we know. This means, in my judgment, that no interpretive institution, ecclesial or academic, can any longer sustain a hegemonic mode of interpretation, so that our capacity for a magisterial or even a broadly based consensus about a pattern of interpretation will be hard to come by. In fact, interpretation is no longer safely in the hands of certified, authorized interpreters, but we are faced with a remarkable pluralism.

Thus I propose a *contextual shift from hegemonic interpretation* (still reflected in the mid-twentieth century by Walther Eichrodt and Gerhard von Rad and more recently by Brevard Childs) *toward a pluralistic interpretive context* (reflected in the texts themselves, in biblical interpreters, and in the culture at large).

Plurality of Testimonies in the Text

We are now able to recognize, against any hypothesis of a unilateral development of Israel's religion or Israel's "God-talk," that the texts themselves witness to a plurality of testimonies concerning God and Israel's life with God.[9] This pluralism is perhaps most clear when one considers the rich array of literary-theological responses to the crisis of the exile. No one response was adequate and no one articulation of Yahweh in exile was sufficient.[10] It is, moreover, clear that the several testimonies to Yahweh, in any particular moment

---

9 See especially Rainer Albertz, *A History of Israelite Religion in the Old Testament Period* 1: *From the Beginnings to the End of the Monarchy* and 2: *From the Exile to the Maccabees* (OTL; Louisville: Westminster/ John Knox, 1994).

10 In addition to Albertz, *A History of Israelite Religion in the Old Testament Period* 2, see also Ralph W. Klein, *Israel in Exile: A Theological Interpretation* (OBT; Philadelphia: Fortress Press, 1979). The fact of the inadequacy of any single articulation of faith is especially clear in the canonical juxtaposition of the Priestly and Deuteronomic traditions.

of Israel's life, were often in profound dispute with one another, disagreeing from the ground up about the "truth" of Yahweh. The several stances of testimony in the Book of Job are evidence of such dispute. In similar fashion, Christopher Seitz has shown how interpretive conflict gives shape to the Book of Jeremiah.[11]

In the end, it is clear that "the final form of the text," in its canonizing process, did not feature a complete hegemonic victory for any interpretive trajectory. As Rainer Albertz has shown, the canonizing process is one of accommodation and compromise.[12] The decision to hold the Priestly and Deuteronomic traditions in tension, accepting and acknowledging both as truth, is a striking evidence of pluralism. Old Testament theology must live with that pluralistic practice of dispute and compromise, so that the texts cannot be arranged in any single or unilateral pattern. It is the process of dispute and compromise itself that constitutes Israel's mode of theological testimony. (Gerhard von Rad saw this pluralism clearly, but he did not point to the constitutive process of dispute and compromise reflected in the pluralism as definitional for Israel's faith.)

Dispute and Accommodation in Interpretation

Our new emerging context of theological interpretation evidences that the pluralism of dispute and accommodation found within the text is matched by a pluralism of dispute and accommodation within the ongoing interpretive enterprise. I have already given attention to the stance of what I have called centrist interpreters and marginated interpreters. Such categories may be too simplistic and reductionist, but the point will be clear.

---

11 Christopher R. Seitz, *Theology in Conflict: Reactions to the Exile in the Book of Jeremiah* (BZAW 176; Berlin: Walter de Gruyter, 1989).

12 Albertz, *A History of Israelite Religion in the Old Testament Period*, 2:468, 481, and passim.

With the proliferation of interpretive methods, and with interpretive voices speaking as never before from a wide range of socio-ecclesial-political-economic contexts, Old Testament theology is now an active process of dispute that does from time to time end in some compromises, accommodations, or acknowledged settlements, albeit provisional ones. Because different interpretations in different contexts—driven by different hopes, fears, and hurts—ask different questions from the ground up, it is clear that there will be no widely accepted "canon within the canon," which is itself a function of hegemonic interpretation. As a consequence, we are now able to see that every interpretation is context-driven and interest-driven to some large extent.[13]

This recognition, now almost a commonplace, is a recent recognition that was not available to previous interpretation. In established, hegemonic interpretation it was possible to imagine (perhaps innocently) that the questions asked of the texts and the methods of interpretive response were obvious, given, and intrinsic to the text. No more so! The ecclesial-academic enterprise of interpretation, like the testimonial process of Israel itself, is a pluralistic one of dispute and accommodation. What is important to recognize is that in such a disputatious interpretive undertaking, every interpretive gesture is a provisional one that must be adjudicated

---

13 Penchansky, *The Politics of Biblical Theology*, has made this clear in a succinct fashion. What he has not made clear is the interest driving postmodern perspectives. I suspect that such perspectives, in rage and resentment against theological authoritarianism, constitute an unwitting lust for Cartesian autonomy. In my judgment that uncritical embrace of autonomy is as costly as the alternative of authoritarianism.

It remains to be seen whether a mode of interpretation is possible that stays clear of both authoritarianism and autonomy. Carl E. Braaten and Robert W. Jenson, eds., *Reclaiming the Bible for the Church* (Grand Rapids: Eerdmans, 1995), seem to me correct on their warnings against autonomous interpretation. But their shrill insistence on "canonical interpretation" sounds profoundly authoritarian to my ears.

yet again. Thus it helps very little to claim high moral ground or high critical ground, or orthodoxy or solemnity of voice or indignation against ideology, because these stances tend to be acknowledged only in privileged contexts.

The theological offer of any particular interpretive voice in any particular interpretive context must make its way in a disputatious process with no evident rules of engagement beyond the readiness to be serious in the dispute.[14] To be sure, there are some elemental agreements in the interpretive process (as there were in the testimonial processes of ancient Israel) that permit the exchange to continue. But these elemental agreements are almost always inchoate. As soon as they are explicated, they take on the shading of more concrete advocacy, which reinvigorates the dispute whereby Israel always arrives afresh at Yahweh.

Postmodern Accounts of Reality

With the demise of Western Christendom and the parallel demise of the old epistemological consensus, it is evident that, beyond the Old Testament and beyond the world of Old Testament interpretation, other very different and very serious accounts of reality are alive in the world. Old Testament theology (or biblical theology or Christian theology) can no longer imagine that it is enunciating a consensus view of reality. This new intellectual situation, widely dubbed "postmodern," has been explicated by Jean-François Lyotard as a situation in which there is no confidence in

---

14 By a disputatious process, I do not mean, as postmodern adherents often seem to suggest, each one doing his or her "own thing." If the matter at issue is serious, then it must be disputed. On a serious matter, no advocate is content simply to let another opinion stand side-by-side unchallenged. The pluralistic, disputatious process requires, in my judgment, a resolve to stay engaged and an ability to listen as well as speak.

metanarratives.[15] In that frame of reference, the Old Testament articulates a metanarrative that, because of its central character Yahweh, is sharply distinguishable from all other metanarratives.[16] In that important regard, moreover, there is a kinship among the various modes of Old Testament theological interpretation.

In my judgment, however, we should not too readily accept Lyotard's verdict about a loss of confidence in metanarratives. I prefer to think that our situation is one of conflict and competition between deeply held metanarratives, which are seldom enunciated and only evidenced in bits and pieces. For example, the metanarrative of ancient Israel is rarely explicated fully in current usage, but rather is presented in bits and pieces in lectionary readings and in scholarly preoccupation with minutiae in the text. In the same way, the dominant metanarrative of military consumerism is seldom articulated in toto, but is exhibited in fragments such as television commercials. As lectionary readings of the Bible appeal to the larger, hidden metanarrative of ancient Israel, so television commercials appeal to the largely (and deliberately?) hidden metanarrative of consumer exploitation.

The important point for our consideration is that the metanarrative of the Old Testament (or of the Bible or of the church) no longer enjoys any hegemonic privilege. It must enter into a pluralistic

---

15 Jean-François Lyotard, *The Postmodern Condition: A Report on Knowledge* (Minneapolis: University of Minnesota Press, 1984).

16 I am not sure whether I should speak of the Old Testament as providing a metanarrative, or as providing the materials out of which a metanarrative might be constructed. I am inclined to the latter. And yet, over against any other metanarrative, all of the metanarratives likely to be constructed out of the materials of the Old Testament are apt to have a striking family resemblance. I prefer to leave the matter open, as it does not affect my argument here. I shall speak simply of metanarrative for purposes of convenience, but with an acknowledgment of my uncertainty, which I do not prejudice by my shorthand usage.

context of interpretation, in order to see what of dispute and accommodation is possible.

These three pluralisms, which displace three long-established hegemonies, seem to me not in question. I am not advocating these displacements, but only insisting that they are powerfully operative and that they constitute the context in which Old Testament theology must now be conducted and will be conducted into the foreseeable future. The loss of hegemony on the part of Western Christendom and on the part of Enlightenment rationality are, in my judgment, irresistible. One need not spend time wishing otherwise. The important point, for the future of Old Testament theology, is how we may assess the shift from a hegemonic to a pluralistic environment.

It is tempting—certainly for this white, Western male—to view the new pluralism as a loss and threat, and to wish for a more ordered circumstance of unacknowledged privilege. In my judgment, however, such a temptation should be resisted. It may well be that our pluralistic context of dispute and accommodation is one of liberation for those who assent to the testimony of the Bible. For in such a context, interpretive work does not have to bear the weight of the entire socioeconomic-political-moral-military establishment. It is possible that the testimony of Israel is to be seen, even in our own time, not as the dominant metanarrative that must give order and coherence across the full horizon of social reality, but as *a subversive protest* and as *an alternative act of vision* that invites criticism and transformation.

Old Testament Theology in Relation to Pluralism

Given this new context in which political and epistemological claims to hegemony seem to be inappropriate, the larger question occurs: Will Old Testament theology be possible at all in time to come? The immediate answer is yes, because people like me will go on doing it and will not be stopped. But we must consider the question more carefully and in relation to the three pluralisms we have identified.

The Metaphor of Testimony

In the work offered here, I have attempted to fashion an approach that honors precisely the variegated nature of the texts themselves. The hallmark of this approach is the governing metaphor of *testimony*. It is not for me to decide whether this attempt has proved successful. I wish nonetheless to make some observations concerning the present work, which I believe are important to any future work in Old Testament theology.

I have proposed that Old Testament theology focuses on Israel's speech about God. The positive warrant for this proposal is that what we have in the Old Testament is speech, nothing else.[17] My approach assumes that speech is constitutive of reality, that words count, that the practitioners of Yahweh are indeed *homo rhetoricus*.[18] Yahweh lives in, with, and under this speech, and in the end depends on Israel's testimony for an access point in the world. This is, of course, a sweeping statement, one that I shall perhaps regret before I am finished.

---

17 In the Old Testament, of course, speech has become writing. I do not minimize the importance of the difference between speech and writing, on which see Walter J. Ong, *Orality and Literacy: The Technologizing of the Word* (London: Methuen, 1982); and Werner H. Kelber, *The Oral and the Written Gospel: The Hermeneutics of Speaking and Writing in the Synoptic Tradition, Mark, Paul, and Q* (Philadelphia: Fortress Press, 1983). The distinction, however, is not important for the point being made here. Thus I refer to "speech" in order to comprehend the entire process of speech-becoming-text.

18 On "rhetorical man," see Richard A. Lanham, *The Motives of Eloquence: Literary Rhetoric in the Renaissance* (New Haven: Yale University Press, 1976) 1–8 and passim.

But the point of settling on speech is that I wish to distinguish Old Testament theology from two temptations that characteristically vex Old Testament interpretation. On the one hand, the Old Testament in the modern world is endlessly vexed by and tempted to historicity; that is, to "what happened."[19] Even Gerhard von Rad, for all his daring, could not escape the modernist trap of history. It is my judgment that Enlightenment modes of history have almost nothing to do with Israel's sense of Yahweh. What "happened" (whatever it may mean) depends on testimony and tradition that will not submit to any other warrant.[20] On the other hand, Old Testament theology is endlessly seduced by the ancient Hellenistic lust for Being, for establishing ontological reference behind the text.[21]

---

19 See Yosef Hayim Yerushalmi, *Zakhor: Jewish History and Jewish Memory* (Seattle: University of Washington Press, 1982), on the crucial distinction between history (as scientifically understood) and memory; and Perdue, *The Collapse of History*, on the problems of positivistic history.

20 The cul-de-sac of "history" as a governing mode of serious theology was made evident by Van Austin Harvey, *The Historian and the Believer: The Morality of Historical Knowledge and Christian Belief* (London: SCM Press, 1967), even though he drew conclusions very different from those I imply here. It is important, for example, that in 1 Corinthians 15 Paul speaks of faith being "futile" (v. 17) if the resurrection has not happened. But his grounding is in explicit testimony (vv. 5–8) and in no other mode of certainty or evidence. Certitude arises in the process of testimony, and not in "objective" recovery of data.

21 It is my judgment that as far as Israel is concerned, "being" is established in and through speech and not behind it. It is not my intention to be anti-ontological. It is rather to insist that whatever might be claimed for ontology in the purview of Israel's speech can be claimed only in and through testimonial utterance. That is, once the testimony of Israel is accepted as true—once one believes what it claims—one has ontology, one has the reality of Yahweh.

But to have the reality of God apart from the testimony of Israel is sure to yield some God other than the Yahweh of Israel. My impression is that the cruciality of speech to reality here is not unlike the claim of the Sophists in ancient Greece; cf. chap. 3, n. 6. This is

Thus, for example, Brevard Childs reaches for "the Real." Perhaps such thinking is inevitable, given our Hellenistic, philosophical inheritance. The truth of the matter, as far as Israel is concerned, is that if one believes the testimony, one is near to reality. And if not, one is not near reality, for the Real is indeed uttered.

Such a construal will not satisfy modernist historicism nor the philosophically minded. It is my impression that to satisfy either of these requires one to give up the venturesome, risky way in which Israel affirms its faith and the equally venturesome and risky way Yahweh lives in the world. It may well be that I have not given correct nuance to these matters because I lack knowledge in the appropriate adjunct disciplines. I have no doubt, nonetheless, that Old Testament theology in the future must do its work in reliance on the lean evidence of utterance.

The metaphor of testimony is particularly suited to the disputatious quality of Old Testament interpretation. In any serious courtroom trial, testimony is challenged by other, competing testimony. In any serious trial, no unchallenged testimony can expect to carry the day easily. Thus I want to insist, against any unilateral rendering of Yahweh's life, or against any systematic portrayal of Yahweh, that Yahweh in the horizon and utterance of Israel is inescapably disputatious and disjunctive.

Testimony for Yahweh is deeply in dispute with other available metanarratives in the contemporary world, as it was in deep dispute with ancient imperial systems and ancient religious alternatives.

---

against the Platonic tradition that claims to shun rhetoric for "being," but in fact only makes that claim as a way to practice very conservative politics, and to preclude challenge that can only be made by rhetoric. I am resistant to the claim of "the real" for the God of the Bible apart from testimonial rhetoric, because such a claim seems to me predictably to issue in and serve conservative if not reactionary politics. See the polemical analysis of the issue by José Miranda, *Being and the Messiah: The Message of St. John* (Maryknoll, N.Y.: Orbis Books, 1973).

Following Fernando Belo, one can see Yahweh as the force of a tradition of order and purity (allied with sociologies of equilibrium) and as the force of a tradition of debt cancellation (allied with sociologies of conflict and revolution).[22] Sufficient texts are given concerning Yahweh to sustain each of these perspectives.

In using the rubrics of "core testimony" and "countertestimony," I have pointed to the undeniable fact that in Israel's own testimony in the text, the "good claims" made for Yahweh as sustainer and transformer are offset and undermined by evidence to the contrary. On many occasions in its canonized testimony, Israel asserts that the sustainer is not always reliable and the transformer is sometimes ineffective. In many texts, but in exemplar fashion in Exod 34:6–7, we have seen that, if the text is to be taken as "witnesses to the real," the ground of dispute is not to be found simply in modern, undisciplined pluralism or in Israel's ancient disputatiousness, but in the very character of Yahweh.[23]

I have insisted that this disputatious quality is definitional for Israel and for Yahweh. The dispute cannot be settled ultimately but only provisionally. In that regard, I believe Old Testament theology is a lively option at the moment of the breakup of the Christian hegemony in the West, for the faith of Israel and the God of Israel precisely refuse the kind of settlement that makes hegemony possible.

The metaphor of testimony is not only verbal, but is embodied as a form of life. In my consideration of the communal, structural, institutional ways in which Israel conducted its testimony, we are

---

22 Fernando Belo, *A Materialist Reading of the Gospel of Mark* (Maryknoll, N.Y.: Orbis Books, 1981). See also Walter Brueggemann, "Trajectories in Old Testament Literature and the Sociology of Ancient Israel," *JBL* 98 (1979) 161–85.

23 On the openness and risk intrinsic to this text, see James L. Crenshaw, "Who Knows What YHWH Will Do? The Character of God in the Book of Joel," *Fortunate the Eyes That See: Essays in Honor of David Noel Freedman* (ed. Astrid B. Beck et al.; Grand Rapids: Eerdmans, 1995) 185–96.

speaking of an embodied community that seeks to live out its testimony and therefore the practice of Yahweh. It seems clear on many counts that the old Cartesian dualism that permits faith to be a reasoned, intellectual activity has failed. Indeed Yahweh, in Yahweh's contradictory self-presentations, is a failure by such norms in any case. The Western hegemonic church, with its sorry record on economics and sexuality, has a long tradition of body-denying in its faith. To be sure, there have been and continue to be vigorous protests against such dualism, but they have not prevailed. And Old Testament theology, in its "idealism," has too often colluded with such denying dualism.[24]

Thus I have insisted that Yahwism in ancient Israel is a matter of communal praxis.[25] We may expect, with emerging pluralism and collapsed hegemony, that the serious, intentional, disciplined practice of Yahweh may take many forms, some local and some larger, some ecclesial and some extraecclesial. Old Testament theology will perhaps on occasion be concrete and bodily enough to authorize such practices in the face of dominant metanarratives that resist such radical embodiment.

Thus, whether I have the nuances correct or not, I anticipate that Old Testament theology, in its attempts to honor the plurality of the text, will have to reckon with

- the cruciality of speech as the mode of Yahweh's actuality,
- the disputatious quality of truth, and

---

24 For a careful critique of such idealistic perspectives in Old Testament scholarship, see Norman K. Gottwald, *The Tribes of Yahweh: A Sociology of the Religion of Liberated Israel, 1250–1050 B.C.E.* (Maryknoll, N.Y.: Orbis Books, 1979) 592–607. On the materiality of biblical faith, see the venturesome extrapolation of Sallie McFague, *The Body of God: An Ecological Theology* (Minneapolis: Fortress Press, 1993).

25 On Old Testament faith as praxis, see Gottwald, *The Tribes of Yahweh*, 700–709 and passim.

- the lived, bodied form of testimonial communities.

These marks, I propose, are congruent with our interpretive situation in the West and present an important contrast to the old, hegemonic forms of Old Testament theology.

Old Testament Theology: Impossible or Unwelcome?

A powerful contemporary opinion holds that Old Testament theology is both an impossibility and an aberration in the wider enterprise of biblical studies. The notion that Old Testament theology is *impossible* stems from the above awareness that the Old Testament itself is profoundly pluralistic, and any notion of Old Testament theology is thought, by definition, to be reductionist, thus riding roughshod over the rich diversity of the text. The notion in Old Testament scholarship that Old Testament theology is *an unwelcome and ignoble project in principle* stems from a very different but related notion. Whereas the notion of impossibility derives from the sense that theological interpretation is inherently reductionist by classifying matters into a neat system, the notion of theological interpretation as an unwelcome aberration, in my view, stems from the sense that theological interpretation is inherently authoritarian, reflective of experiences or impressions of an ecclesial interpretive authority that was coercive in its requirements. Indeed, a long history exists of wounding theological interpretation that is both reductionist and coercive.

Back in the days of a unified historical criticism, scholarship in general seemed to tolerate a gap between critical conclusions and theological assumptions, a gap hidden by slippery language (especially about "history") and seldom exposed. Thus one had the odd result of rigorous critical scholarship that ostensibly yielded a most innocent theological interpretation. It is a curious, and in my view unfortunate, mark of current scholarship that many scholars have moved beyond historical criticism in its older modes, but have moved into the kinds of rhetorical and literary studies that are skeptical if not resistant to theological interpretation. These recent studies often are marked with insightful observations of an artistic and aesthetic kind about the strategies of the text, so that attention is given to everything except the "testimony" *to Yahweh* that is offered in the text.[26]

It is my impression that such resistance to theological claim about the character of Yahweh as the God to whom Israel bears witness is not rooted in anything about the testimony as such. It is rooted, rather, in old wounds of reductionism and coercion, wounds that are kept hidden or are denied in the name of scientific distancing. My impression, further, is that this aversion to theological interpretation occurs especially among Roman Catholic scholars who have suffered at the hands of an imposing, insistent magisterium, and among scholars with a Protestant upbringing in which coercive social control was confused with the God given in the testimony of Israel.

I have no negative judgment to make about scholarship that stays clear of theological interpretation because of past oppressive experiences at the hands of ecclesial interpretive communities, though I think one would be better served if such scholars shared that shaping personal reality in their work. The greater problem, it appears to me, is that such scholars tend to regard Enlightenment rationality with a kind of naive innocence, as though that perspective were not as ideology-laden, and ultimately as reductionist and coercive, as any ecclesial interpretation could ever be.[27]

---

26 See the protest of Jack Miles, *God: A Biography* (New York: Knopf, 1995), against Enlightenment positivistic scholarship that can speak of everything except Yahweh.

27 Thus Hans-Georg Gadamer, *Truth and Method* (New York: Seabury Press, 1975) 239–40, can speak of the Enlightenment "prejudice against prejudice itself."

It is my hope that I have modeled a responsible way of doing Old Testament theological interpretation that is a genuine alternative to these stereotypical modes that so deeply offend and so profoundly wound. It is my expectation that Old Testament theological interpretation that is viable in our new interpretive situation need not and dare not be reductionist. That is why I have focused on disputatious testimony that refuses closure. In parallel fashion, Old Testament theological interpretation, in my judgment, need not and dare not be coercive, because it does not aim at a consensus conclusion. It aims, rather, at an ongoing, contested conversation about the character of Yahweh.

It is a great problem for Old Testament scholars who, for reasons of their own, are resistant to what they regard as theological interpretation to imagine that the character of God lives "outside the text," that is, has metaphysical substance. But that objection in principle imposes a dualism of text/nontext that passionate testimony never entertains. Thus I am content to have theological interpretation stay inside the text—to refrain from either historical or ontological claim extrinsic to the text—but to take the text seriously as testimony and to let it have its say alongside other testimonies, including the testimony of Enlightenment rationality that, with like force, affirms and precludes. It is my hope that if consideration of Israel's God-talk can be separated from hegemonic administration that has largely monopolized that God-talk, then Old Testament scholars might be free to consider this testimony also outside the hegemonic rationality of the Enlightenment. In my judgment, we are at a moment in Old Testament theology when we might reconsider the categories in which the power of Israel's testimonial utterance might be reconsidered, apart from every heavy-handed enforcer, ecclesial as well as academic, confessional as well as rationalistic.

The Metanarrative of Military Consumerism

Our context within which to consider the viability of Old Testament theology is the wider social context of the West, where another metanarrative is more powerful and compelling. I have already suggested a correction to Lyotard's notion of no confidence in metanarratives, to suggest instead competing metanarratives that exercise enormous power, even if they are kept strangely hidden. Pluralism in the public arena does not mean "anything goes." Such a notion of unmitigated freedom is itself a function of military consumerism. In reality, in any particular circumstance, public or personal, we are not confronted by a myriad of limitless options, but we are met with only a few choices, each of which is situated in a (often unrecognized) metanarrative.[28]

It is my judgment that the dominant metanarrative of Western society, and therefore the primary alternative to Israel's Yahwistic construal of reality, is military consumerism. I shall premise my discussion here on that basis. (In other social settings one might focus on some other primary alternative to Israel's Yahwistic construal of reality.) By "military consumerism" I refer to a construal of the world in which individual persons are reckoned as the primary units of meaning and reference, and individual persons, in unfettered freedom, are authorized (self-authorized) to pursue well-being, security, and happiness as they choose.

This metanarrative has, as its "consumer" component, the conviction that well-being, security, and happiness are the result of getting, having, using, and consuming, activities that may be done without restraint or limit, even at the expense of others. This

---

28   Alasdair MacIntyre, *Whose Justice? Which Rationality?* (Notre Dame, Ind.: University of Notre Dame Press, 1988); and *Three Rival Versions of Moral Enquiry: Encyclopedia, Genealogy, and Tradition* (Notre Dame, Ind.: University of Notre Dame Press, 1990), suggests that there are three fundamental options.

construal of reality has its "military" component in the conviction that having a disproportion of whatever it takes to enjoy well-being, security, and happiness is appropriate, and that the use of force, coercion, or violence, either to secure or to maintain a disproportion, is completely congruent with this notion of happiness.

This construal of reality, moreover, exercises a totalizing effect among us by its technological availability and by its capacity to control public imagination through the media. This metanarrative is so massive and so compelling that it largely defines the thinkable, imaginable options, holding together, as it does, enormous freedom of a certain kind with a tight conformity that precludes any serious challenge to the current, disproportionate deployment of power, goods, and access.

In these broad strokes, I may have caricatured the dominant metanarrative; that is not my intention. I believe that this is a rough portrayal of our true ideological situation. Many "users" and interpreters of the Old Testament, moreover, find it altogether possible to take bits and pieces of Israel's testimony in the Old Testament and accommodate them to the main claims of the metanarrative of military consumerism, thus removing these bits and pieces from their own habitat in Israel's testimony, and thereby completely distorting them.

It is in this ideological context that we ask our question: Is Old Testament theology possible in the wider social context of the West, where another metanarrative is more powerful and compelling? In other words, can the world be imagined in any sustained way according to Israel's testimony, when the imaginative power of military consumerism is so overwhelming? The answer to that question is not obvious, and surely a positive answer is not easy. If Old Testament theology—that is, Israel's characteristic construal of the world around the character of Yahweh—is to be credible in authorizing an alternative life in the world, then I suggest that an interpretive, interpreting community must attend to the issues that stand between this construal of reality and the claims of military consumerism.

Israel's testimony invites "the court" into a world of *undomesticated holiness,* marked by staggering sovereignty and inexplicable fidelity, but given in ways that are disjunctive and disruptive. Such an offer testifies against the hegemonic vision of military consumerism, which imagines that the world can be secured, explained, mastered, and controlled, and which makes convenient common cause with the domesticated divinity of bourgeois Christianity. Israel invites residence in a world beset by ambiguity and unsettlement, rooted in the life of the central Character.

Israel's testimony invites "the court" into a world of *originary generosity* in which gifts are inexplicably given for "more than all we can ask or imagine" (Eph 3:20). Such an offer testifies against the grudging inclination of military consumerism, which concludes that no gifts are given, that there is no generosity, that everything is quid pro quo, and that one must have self-sufficient resources in order to get more. Israel invites residence in a world saturated by an inexplicable generosity, rooted only in the life of the central Character.

Israel's testimony invites "the court" into a world of *indefatigable possibility,* in which promises are endlessly enacted beyond all visible circumstance, and in which new waves of promise are being uttered that permit passionate hope beyond every explanatory option. Such an offer tells against the closed-down world of military consumerism that imagines there are no more promises to be kept and no more words to be uttered, and so concludes in a self-destructive, world-destructive despair. Israel invites residence in a world overrun with freighted promises that dazzle in their fulfillments, and that sustain in the long, dry season between; promises and possibilities rooted only in the resolve of the central Character.

Israel's testimony invites "the court" into a world of *open-ended interaction,* a covenantal exchange that continually redeploys power between the strong and the weak and that even invites demanding, insistent interventions against Yahweh. Such an offer of a lively covenantal existence testifies against the fixed, fated world of military consumerism, in which the poor only become poorer, the rich become richer, and together the rich and the poor end in a paralysis of pride, despair, and a futile death. Israel invites residence in a world that is genuinely open for giving and receiving, for the full exchange of value in trust and confidence, an openness rooted in the life of the central Character, who can on occasion be on the receiving end and often on the giving end.

Israel's testimony invites "the court" into a world of *genuine neighborliness*, in which members in a community share without fear and practice justice that assures well-being for every member of the community. Such an invitation to community testifies against the harsh, definitional selfishness of military consumerism, in which every neighbor is reduced to a usable commodity, where the process of commoditization eventually empties even the subject of the individual of all human possibility. Israel invites residence in a world of caring and sharing, in which members know that something counts more than the surface offers of well-being, security, and happiness that have no human depth.

In rough outline, Israel's testimony yields a world as deeply opposed to military consumerism as it is to every other alternative metanarrative that lacks the markings of the central Character. It is not a given that a world marked by undomesticated holiness, originary generosity, indefatigable possibility, open-ended interaction, and genuine neighborliness is more compelling than other metanarratives, for the chief alternative among us does make some surface promises that it can keep. Only in the presence of the richer, more dense metanarrative of Yahwism can the inadequacy of the dominant metanarrative be observed. And where the metanarrative of Yahwism is not fully and courageously voiced, the dominant metanarrative appears as the only available one. I believe that this inability or refusal to voice the metanarrative made possible in Israel's testimony has, in no small way, permitted the metanarrative of military consumerism to dominate by default.

It is the task of Old Testament theology, set in the large arena of competing alternatives, to evidence the ways in which a counter metanarrative may have authority. There is nothing inherently or especially reductionist or coercive about this alternative wrought of Israel's testimony. Israel uttered this construal of reality to itself, to its young, and to outsiders, because Israel believed the issues were as serious as life and death. It is possible, here and there in odd and local ways, that this construal of reality takes on authority. That finally is what is at stake in Old Testament theology.

THE CONSTITUTIVE POWER
OF ISRAEL'S TESTIMONY

In my discussion, I have staked a great deal on the claim that the testimony of Israel is fundamentally constituted by *concrete utterance*, which is generative of social reality. This is an enormous claim; I believe, however, it is of interest not only for the exposition I have offered. It is equally important, in my judgment, for the future of Old Testament theology more generally, as disestablishment leaves biblical interpretation without many of its accustomed institutional, sociopolitical supports. I suggest that concrete utterance is more elemental to Israel's embrace and explication of Yahweh than are the two accustomed claims of history and ontology.

Concerning history, I suggest that the question of what "happened" is now hopelessly intertwined with positivistic historicism, which intends, characteristically, to remove what is awkward or scandalous (and normative) in utterances-become-texts. Utilization of historical research as an instance of theological skepticism seems to me evident in the current rage to date everything in the Old Testament late. Thus: "It is late, therefore it did not really happen, therefore it could hardly be authoritative." Some such inclination appears to be at work in the "Third Quest" of the "Jesus Seminar."[29]

Conversely, in a reaction against such debunking historicism, others are making a positive effort to reach outside the text to get at the "really real"—at the God who is outside and beyond the text,

---

29 On the "Jesus Seminar," see the fine forum offered in *TToday* 52 (1995) 1–97, especially Marcus J. Borg, "The Historian, the Christian, and Jesus," 6–16, and Howard Clark Kee, "A Century of Quests for the Culturally Compatible Jesus," 17–28. See also Luke Timothy Johnson, *The Real Jesus* (San Francisco: Harper, 1996).

so that the text references beyond itself.[30] This push, it appears to me, is pursued in the conviction that the utterance-become-text itself is not adequate, so that utterance spoken loudly enough and in capital letters becomes metaphysics.

Both of these temptations to want more (or less in the case of dismissive historicism) than the text seem to me hopeless enterprises and surely ones that Old Testament theology must eschew. To be sure, compared to confident historical reconstructionism and to conventional metaphysical claims, utterance-become-text seems a thin basis for life in the world. It is my judgment, however, that in the ancient world of Israel's utterance it was enough for the most yielding of Israelites.[31] Moreover, in our own time and place, I propose that we must consider carefully whether theological interpretation may trust the utterance enough to receive the God given in the text, for finally "history" or "ontology," as starting points for theological interpretation, will appeal to utterance-become-text as its pivot point.[32] I suggest that what we must examine is not how

---

30 See Brevard S. Childs, *Biblical Theology of the Old and New Testaments: Theological Reflection on the Christian Bible* (Minneapolis: Fortress Press, 1993) 20 and passim; and more recently see Childs, "On Reclaiming the Bible for Christian Theology," *Reclaiming the Bible for the Church* (ed. Carl E. Braaten and Robert W. Jenson; Grand Rapids: Eerdmans, 1995) 1–17. Karl Barth, *Church Dogmatics* 1/1 (Edinburgh: T. & T. Clark, 1975), focuses on the word as testimony in a way congruent with what I am suggesting. But Barth could not finally let word as utterance (proclamation) stand apart from a threefold notion of word (Jesus, Bible, proclamation), which for him in the end is more "being" than speech.

31 My impression is that those who "yielded," who found this uttered world compelling, did so not because of some prior religious disposition, but because of desperation wrought by their real-life, sociopolitical situation. That is, the utterance "made sense" of nonsensical situations of deathliness.

32 See Walter Brueggemann, *Biblical Perspectives on Evangelism: Living in a Three-Storied Universe* (Nashville: Abingdon Press, 1993) 94–128.

Israel could rely on such a lean resource, but why that utterance now seems to us so untrustworthy and flimsy.

In making this claim I refer to Israel's characteristic utterance, which, over much time and in many circumstances, has a recognizable cadence. I do not refer to any attempt to locate "original" or early utterance, but only reliable, recurring utterance, which is the substance of Old Testament theology. This recognizable, peculiar utterance is such that for one of its adherents, only a few words need be heard to complete the utterance; if some words cannot be heard, they can be filled in by those who know the way this utterance works. The identifiability of this utterance is not unlike hearing one's own language on the street in a location where another language is normally spoken. It takes only a little overhearing to recognize the pattern of speech of one's native tongue and to have its utterance be a welcoming, sense-making moment. Having recognized the familiarity of the utterance, it is then possible as well to recognize and appreciate the variations and deviations from the familiar, which we may assume are enacted with great intentionality. At some important level, faith consists in a willingness to live in the world of this utterance, and to accept as reliable its speech as testimony.

Such speech—spoken regularly, in season and out of season—recruits persons into this community and into its faith (that is, its construal of reality; cf. Deut 6:4–9; Ps 78:5–8) by a *pedagogy of saturation*. This speech is summons, demand, assurance, and invitation to belong to this community of utterance and to the world uttered by this community, including the God at the center of this uttered world. Adherents to Yahweh, in the Old Testament, are those who accept this characteristic testimony as a valid articulation of reality, on which they are prepared to act.

In the context of this community, which recruits, nurtures, disciplines, and admonishes its members and candidates for membership, these utterances are indeed constitutive of reality. Israel regularly speaks a particular world into availability. Its polemical speech, moreover, intends at the same time to nullify worlds it dismisses as false, unreliable, and deathly.

In making this claim, it is important to recognize that there is, outside speech, no objectively given world that stands as a measuring rod of reality, whereby one can test to see if Israel is "realistic."[33] In its iconoclastic insistence, Israel holds that such worlds that have come to be regarded as given over time are in fact only other spoken worlds, spoken so long, so authoritatively, and so credibly that they appear to be given. Thus Israel's testimony about a world with Yahweh at its center intends to debunk and nullify all other proposed worlds that do not have Yahweh at their center. This testimony undertaken persistently by Israel is not neutral or descriptive, but it is thoroughly and pervasively partisan advocacy. This partisan advocacy, moreover, is generative and constitutive of a new world, when "recruits" sign on to this world of utterance. In signing on, such recruits and members at the same time depart other worlds that are based in other normative utterances (cf. Josh 24:23).

This peculiar world of utterance, with Yahweh at its center, has a quality of constancy to it through time, and it is this constancy that constitutes the material of Old Testament theology. Two features of this constancy are in deep tension. On the one hand, the Yahwistic constancy of Israel's testimony is deeply laden with ideological freight. This is especially evident in the "Yahweh alone" party associated with the Deuteronomic traditions, a stance

---

33 I refer to the temptation to foundationalism. While more philosophically inclined theological interpretation may make a case for foundationalism, I do not see any opening for it in core Old Testament claims as such. It is the great force of Old Testament testimony to Yahweh (as well as its great problematic) that utterance of Yahweh is not measured by previous historical or ontological reality.

intolerant of variation or deviation.[34] That "Yahweh alone" party provided a rhetorical world that not only is insistently Yahwistic, but also tends to be deeply patriarchal and capable of sanctioning violence against all deviations from its ideology.

On the other hand, having recognized its ideological heavy-handedness, we must also recognize that Yahwistic constancy has a relentless quality of elusiveness. Thus the Yahweh who is authoritarian also turns out to be the Yahweh who is beyond domestication and imprisonment.[35] This elusive quality seems to be almost inherent in the notion of Israel's testimonial utterance, which is marked by teasing ambiguity, expressed in metaphors that cannot be flattened to precision. In the end this elusive quality is desconstructive of the ideological rigor noted above, so that when Yahweh is portrayed in savage ideology, one can regularly notice hints to the contrary.

This quality of constancy as both *ideology* and *elusiveness* is a rich interpretive invitation. I suppose, in the end, we must make a crucial judgment about whether ideology or elusiveness has the last word.[36] In my own reading, I find that no ideological statement of

---

34 On the "Yahweh alone" party, see Morton Smith, *Palestinian Parties and Politics That Shaped the Old Testament* (New York: Columbia University Press, 1971); and Martin Rose, *Der Ausschliesschlichkeitsanspruch Jahwes; Deuteronomische Schultheologie und die Volksfrommigkeit in der Späten Konigszeit* (BWANT 6; Stuttgart: W. Kohlhammer Verlag, 1975).

35 In a study of Micah, my student Timothy K. Beal, "System and Speaking Subject in the Hebrew Bible: Reading for Divine Abjection," *Biblical Interpretation* 2 (1994) 171–89, has shown how the ideological critique of Julia Kristeva in fact misses the intention of the text to allow Yahweh considerable instability, certainly more instability than is welcomed by harsh, ideological critics of the text.

36 Those who regard the text as ideological are likely to tilt toward skepticism, and those who find in the text elusiveness will move in a fideistic direction. But fideism also is open to reductionism as is skepticism. There is no "answer in the back of the book." I insist only that

Yahweh is permitted finally to prevail, always being undermined by elusiveness. But some other readers, perhaps wounded by authoritarian interpretation as I have not been, will find that ideology finally wins out over the elusiveness. Or it may be simply that the issue of ideology and elusiveness is the very marking of constancy that belongs to Yahweh, who is endlessly responsive and available and at the same time intransigently sovereign. That unresolved, and perhaps unresolvable, issue is precisely what is so compelling and so maddening about Old Testament theology.

The constancy and generativity of this characteristic utterance of Israel has a profound density to it, which is available only to its committed practitioners. This density means that the Yahwistic testimony of Israel is deeply coded, so that there is always allusion and reference within an utterance that refers to another utterance.[37] The density is not simply moral or cognitive, but it has a practical, material aspect that pertains to the lived, public, institutional life of Israel. As a result, any hearing of these utterances that seeks to keep them separated from their radical socioeconomic counterparts is a mishearing. Thus serious hearing of such utterance entails bodily practice in the disciplines and freedoms arising from the utterance—and the greatest of these is neighbor love.

Israel's elemental reliance on utterance has characteristically had rough going in the world. It is perhaps this odd quality of utterance, nearly ideological, characteristically elusive, that marks Israelite oddity in the world, an oddity that must be resisted if

---

skeptical-as-ideological propensities have no privilege in interpretation. I suspect that polemics between skepticism and fideism are misguided, because the real issue is between ideological reductionism and openness to elusiveness. It is not difficult to align fideism and skepticism together around questions of reductionism and elusiveness.

37 The basic study in intertextuality is by Michael Fishbane, *Biblical Interpretation in Ancient Israel* (Oxford: Clarendon Press, 1985). See above my discussion of an intertextual perspective, pp. 78–80.

control of the world is to be secured.[38] Here useful appeal may be made to Jacques Ellul's phrase, "The Humiliation of the Word."[39] Already in 1967 in *The Technological Society*, Ellul had considered the dehumanizing power of modern technology.[40] His book advances the analysis by its insistence that manipulated image has displaced speech in the modern world, in the service of technological control.[41]

It is not my purpose here to review or assess Ellul's thesis about the word. Rather I suggest that theology in general and Old Testament theology in particular have either participated in "the humiliation of the word," or at least have been seduced by it, so that there has been a deep yearning for something more (or something other) than the utterance itself, either historical or ontological. My argument is an insistence that utterance is all we have—utterance as testimony—and that utterance as testimony is enough, as it was for the community of Israel.

---

38 On the oddity and the overcoming of oddity under the pressure of universalism, see John Murray Cuddihy, *The Ordeal of Civility: Freud, Marx, Levi-Strauss and the Jewish Struggle with Modernity* (New York: Basic Books, 1974). Cuddihy proposes that "Freudian slips" are a peculiarly Jewish phenomenon when suppressed Jewishness will out. On such a notion, I suggest that the Bible is full of such "slips," some on the lips of Yahweh.

39 Jacques Ellul, *The Humiliation of the Word* (Grand Rapids: Eerdmans, 1988).

40 Jacques Ellul, *The Technological Society* (New York: Alfred A. Knopf, 1965).

41 See also Neil Postman, *Amusing Ourselves to Death: Public Discourse in the Age of Show Business* (New York: Penguin Books, 1985); and *Conscientious Objections: Stirring Up Trouble about Language, Technology, and Education* (London: Heinemann, 1988); see also the more fundamental study of Eugen Rosenstock-Huessy, *Speech and Reality* (Norwich, Vt.: Argo Books, 1970), who comments on the "pathology of speech" in modern life.

This recognition, that utterance is all we have and is enough, assures that Israel's knowledge of God is endlessly elusive, under challenge, and in dispute. Israel thereby refuses the kind of certitude that either historical positivism or theological positivism can give. Therefore, I propose that serious theological readers of the Old Testament are either adherents to and practitioners of the world rendered in this utterance, or they are candidates and potential recruits into this uttered world. Those who are adherents are endlessly under challenge, for this world must be lived in the presence of other worlds, also given in utterance. It is because the challenge to the adherents is incessant that the utterance of Israel includes countertestimony. In like fashion, candidates and potential recruits for this uttered world have not yet decided about the reliability of this utterance, and do indeed have alternative utterances and alternative worlds—that is, alternative metanarratives—available to them. This utterance of Israel is not a dictator. It will not impose its will. It can only issue its summons and its invitation, and await a decision that is always to be made yet again. When an affirmative decision is made, a real world of ontological substance follows.

SOME PERVASIVE ISSUES

In the foreseeable future, Old Testament theology (a) lives in a pluralistic world without hegemonic privilege; and (b) is utterance-dependent. Having situated our future work in Old Testament theology in this way, which is in profound contrast with the long Enlightenment period of scholarship, I wish to return briefly to the four pervasive issues that I have flagged as elemental and enduring concerns for our continuing work.[42] I here ask about these issues in a world that is pluralistic and utterance-dependent.

Old Testament Theology in Relation to Historical Criticism

No doubt Brevard Childs is correct in his contention that the relationship between Old Testament theology and historical criticism is of crucial importance to any advance in Old Testament theology.[43] Equally, there is no doubt that historical criticism, broadly construed, is crucial for responsible biblical theology, especially Reformed versions of it, as Gerhard Ebeling has insisted.[44] One cannot undo the long and complex history that has held criticism and theological exposition together and in tension. One cannot,

---

42 On these four pervasive questions, see pp. 102–14.

43 Brevard S. Childs, "Critical Reflections on James Barr's Understanding of the Literal and the Allegorical," *JSOT* 46 (1990) 3–9, and again in "On Reclaiming the Bible for Christian Theology," *Reclaiming the Bible for the Church* (ed. Carl E. Braaten and Robert W. Jenson; Grand Rapids: Eerdmans, 1995) 1–17.

44 Gerhard Ebeling, "The Significance of the Critical Historical Method for Church and Theology in Protestantism," *Word and Faith* (London: SCM Press, 1963) 17–61. See Childs, *Biblical Theology of the Old and New Testaments: Theological Reflection on the Christian Bible* (Minneapolis: Fortress Press, 1993) 6–9, for his comment on the accent of Ebeling.

moreover, wish as a contemporary expositor to abandon the intellectual restraints and resources of one's time and place. Thus I take it as a truism that Old Testament theological interpretation must be seriously engaged with criticism, and any serious student of Old Testament theology cannot retreat into a "safe" fideism because he or she fears the results of critical inquiry.

But Ebeling's insistence, in my judgment, does not touch the real issues that must now be addressed. Ebeling is concerned to insist that Christian faith has real historical roots in what "has happened," and he uses the term *historical* in that way. In fact, however, the term *historical* with reference to "what happened" is not at all the way that the word has come to be used in "historical criticism" in much Old Testament scholarship. While agreeing with Ebeling's general point, I insist that what is appropriate as criticism in relation to Old Testament theology is to be measured by two criteria: (a) an approach that is congruent with the material of the text itself; and (b) an approach that is congruent with the intellectual environment in which exposition is to be done.

The conclusion to which I am drawn is that the enormous apparatus of high historical criticism that reached its zenith in the nineteenth century and continued its dominance well into the twentieth century is not, in the first instant, of primary relevance to theological exposition at the end of the twentieth century. By such a conclusion, I do not intend any appeal to an anti-intellectual fideism; I appeal rather to criticism that is congruent in the two ways suggested. In drawing this conclusion, I only reflect what in practice has turned out to be the case for a great number of responsible scholars at the present moment, namely, that scholars have moved well beyond the critical categories that have come to represent historical criticism.[45]

---

45 Concerning the "new criticisms," reference should be made especially to sociological, literary, rhetorical, and canonical criticism. Of these,

In my judgment, historical criticism (by which I shall refer to the entire Enlightenment enterprise that came to be associated with Julius Wellhausen and that now seems to reappear as neo-Wellhausianism) was committed to a Cartesian program that was hostile (in effect if not in intention) to the main theological claims of the text. That is, historical criticism did not confine itself to consideration of the specific historical locus of texts (which seems to be Ebeling's concern), but operated with naturalistic assumptions, so that everything could and must be explained, without reference to any theological claim. The outcome is a "history of religion" that not only resists theological metanarrative, but resists any notion of Yahweh as an agent in Israel's life.

I fully recognize that to claim "Yahweh as agent" is enormously problematic.[46] It is problematic, however, only when interpretation is conducted according to the assumptions of Enlightenment rationality that, in principle, resist every theological claim. In its avoidance of fideism, criticism slipped over into skepticism so that, in the words of Jack Miles, everything could be talked about except Yahweh. It is evident that such skeptical criticism is indispensable when one focuses on uncritical fundamentalism of "the first naiveté."[47] That work, on the grounds of Enlightenment rationality,

---

the sociological is still most closely linked to the older historical criticism. Brevard Childs insists that canonical criticism is not just one more method, but is in fact a theological perspective. See the review of current "options" in Steven L. McKenzie and Stephen R. Haynes, *To Each Its Own Meaning: An Introduction to Biblical Criticisms and Their Application* (Louisville: Westminster/John Knox, 1993).

46 To refer to "Yahweh as agent" reintroduces the whole vexed issue of a "God who acts." For a review of the issue, see Thomas F. Tracy, *God, Action, and Embodiment* (Grand Rapids: Eerdmans, 1984).

47 The phrase is from Paul Ricoeur. See Mark I. Wallace, *The Second Naiveté: Barth, Ricoeur, and the New Yale Theology* (Macon, Ga.: Mercer University Press, 1990).

has been done well and continues to be done well in most U.S. theological schools.

The problem is that such Enlightenment positivism no longer pertains in any critical discipline. The emergence of hermeneutical reflection is now a major dimension of any critical undertaking, and Ebeling himself defines criticism in this way: "Everything depends on the critical historical method being freed from this mistaken curtailment to a mere technical tool and being understood in such a way as to include in itself the whole of the hermeneutic process."[48] Thus what is required in a new, antipositivistic intellectual climate is a criticism that is not thinly positivistic, but open to the density of social and rhetorical processes that generate social reality beyond our "realism."[49]

I suggest that in a new settlement still to be worked out between criticism and interpretation, three considerations are pertinent:

1. Serious energy needs to be given to discern what of the older historical criticism is to be retained and how it is to be used. There is much in the history of the literature and perhaps in the history of religion that still needs to be valued, even though almost every old "consensus" opinion is now under heavy assault. The challenge in retaining learning from the older historical criticism is to do so without a hidden commitment to the theological skepticism that seemed endlessly to accompany that criticism, but was not a necessary part of a critical perspective. There may be a place for skepticism, but it should be explicit along with its grounds, and not surreptitiously taken along with critical judgment.

---

48 Ebeling, "The Significance of the Critical Historical Method," 50.
49 Reference might be made here to Richard R. Niebuhr, *Resurrection and Historical Reason: A Study of Theological Method* (New York: Charles Scribner's Sons, 1957); and W. B. Gallie, "The Historical Understanding," *History and Theory* (ed. George H. Nadel; Middletown, Conn.: Wesleyan University Press, 1977) 149–202.

2. There is much in emerging methods—sociological (including the new archaeology) and rhetorical—that can be valued, because these methods allow both for the density of social processes coded in the text and for the generative, constitutive power of the textual utterance. These methods in general, in my judgment, meet the expectation of Ebeling's notion of criticism, but they do in principle commit to skeptical rationality.

3. Since the complete domination of scholarship by historical criticism in the nineteenth century, it has been assumed, almost without question, that criticism is the lead figure, taking the initiative in the scholarly process, and that theological interpretation must follow along in the categories established by criticism. Certainly in a period of high positivism, this shape to the relationship is inevitable.

With the emergence of a hermeneutical dimension in criticism that has moved beyond sheer positivism, this widely assumed relationship might be reexamined and reordered.[50] For example, an accent on the disputatious quality in Israel's theological rhetoric might lead to a criticism of documents that resists Enlightenment fragmentation, which seeks to dissolve all of the odd tensions and abrasions in the text. Indeed, having moved beyond positivism into an entertainment of the density of the text, we may observe emerging methods that are willing to allow for a theological dimension that moves in a direction of a "second naiveté."

The real issue in the relationship between interpretation and criticism is to be aware that fideism and skepticism are twin temptations, and that criticism is an effort to be thoughtful in a way

---

50 Above all, see Hans-Georg Gadamer, *Truth and Method* (New York: Seabury Press, 1975). Note especially his accent on language, 345–491. As Gadamer seeks to refute the *knowledge-claims* of positivism, so Martin Buber in his dialogic articulation of reality seeks to overturn the *being-claims* of Cartesianism.

that does not permit fideism and that does not require skepticism. In much "scientific" study of the Old Testament, it is generally assumed that skepticism is much more intellectually respectable than is fideism. With the demise of positivism, that unstated but widespread assumption might well be reconsidered. Skepticism, often voiced as hostility to theological claim, is in fact not a given element in responsible intellectual inquiry.[51] What passes for uncommitted objectivity in Old Testament study, moreover, is often a thinly veiled personal hostility to religious authority, which is displaced on the interpretive task as though such hostility is an intellectual virtue. No doubt an oppressive fideism and a hostile skepticism endlessly evoke and feed each other. We may now be at a moment when totalizing fideism is exposed as inadequate and when skeptical positivism is seen to be equally inadequate, when a genuinely thoughtful criticism can engage the density and depth of the text, which is available neither to fideism nor to skepticism.

Old Testament Theology in Relation to the New Testament and to Church Theology

Old Testament theology has been characteristically a Christian enterprise, for it is a Christian, as distinct from a Jewish, propensity to think in large, systematic theological categories.[52] And

---

51 See the powerful critique of liberal skepticism as it has occupied the center of academic activity in the United States: George Marsden, *The Soul of the American University: From Protestant Establishment to Established Non-belief* (Oxford: Oxford University Press, 1994). For a very different posture toward the issue, see Martin E. Marty, "Committing the Study of Religion in Public," *JAAR* 57 (1989) 1–22.

52 See Jon D. Levenson, "Why Jews Are Not Interested in Biblical Theology," *The Hebrew Bible, the Old Testament, and Historical Criticism: Jews and Christians in Biblical Studies* (Louisville: Westminster/John Knox, 1993) 33–61; and Childs, *Biblical Theology of the Old and New Testaments*, 25–26, on "Jewish theology."

because the recurring categories of Old Testament theology have been determined and practiced by Christian interpreters, it is not surprising that Old Testament theology has been conducted on the assumption that the Old Testament is integrally and exclusively aimed at the New Testament. Because interpretation has been conducted on this assumption, moreover, it is altogether understandable that Old Testament theology should have become a major contributor to supersessionism, whereby Jewish religious claims are overridden in the triumph of Christian claims. This way of thinking is evident in the notorious statement of Rudolf Bultmann that the Old Testament is "a history of failure," and most recently in the assertion of Brevard Childs that the two Testaments "bear witnesses to Jesus Christ."[53] Such a way of presenting the Old Testament proceeds as if the community of Judaism was only an interim community, which existed until the New Testament and then withered into nonexistence and insignificance.[54]

---

53 Rudolf Bultmann, "The Significance of the Old Testament for the Christian Faith," *The Old Testament and Christian Faith* (ed. Bernhard W. Anderson; London: SCM Press, 1964) 8–35; Childs, *Biblical Theology of the Old and New Testaments*, 78 and passim. For two Jewish perspectives, see Levenson, "Why Jews Are Not Interested in Biblical Theology," and M. H. Goshen-Gottstein, "Tanakh Theology: The Religion of the Old Testament and the Place of Jewish Biblical Theology," *Ancient Israelite Religion: Essays in Honor of Frank Moore Cross* (ed. Patrick D. Miller Jr. et al.; Philadelphia: Fortress Press, 1989) 617–44

54 The Old Testament, for the most part, disappears as Childs seeks to do "biblical theology" under the aegis of christological claims. Rolf Rendtorff, *Canon and Theology* (OBT; Minneapolis: Fortress Press, 1993), has most seriously suggested a recognition of Jewish reality in considering the task of Old Testament theology. Reference will usefully be made to the title of Rendtorff's recent *Festschrift, Die Hebräische Bibel und ihre zweifache Nachgeschichte* (ed. Erhard Blum et al.; Neukirchen-Vluyn: Neukirchener Verlag, 1990).

It should be evident to the reader by now that I do not subscribe to such a view, but understand the relation of the Old to the New Testament in a very different way. Since the church rejected the views of Marcion in the second century C.E., it has been impossible in Christian theology to dissolve the Old Testament into the New. The church, in a programmatic decision, held on to the Old Testament as scripture because the Old Testament affirmed something definitional for Christianity that was not elsewhere affirmed and that Christians dared not lose.

Over time, various attempts have been made to identify the relationship between the Old Testament and the New Testament in Christian theology, especially under the rubrics of promise-fulfillment, law-gospel, salvation history, and topology.[55] Each of these rubrics offers something of importance. It is equally clear, however, that none of these rubrics nor all of them together catch what is decisive in the Old Testament for the New Testament and for Christian faith. It is not easy or obvious to identify what must be retained from the Old Testament for the truth of Christianity. But surely in some sense it is the "scandal of particularity," by which the Creator of heaven and earth has sojourned with the Israelite community and has self-disclosed in the odd and concrete ways of Jewishness.[56] The Jewish markings of elusiveness, materiality, and concreteness that belong to the very character of Yahweh are what Marcionite Christianity always wants to scuttle. It is the purpose of Christian Old Testament theology, I judge, to pay particular attention to these aspects of Old Testament testimony, which are most problematic for Hellenized, Enlightenment Christianity.

---

55 For an older but helpful review of the issues, see A. H. J. Gunneweg, *Understanding the Old Testament* (OTL; London: SCM Press, 1978).

56 Paul M. Van Buren, *Discerning the Way: A Theology of the Jewish-Christian Reality* 1: *Discerning the Way* (San Francisco: Harper and Row, 1987), has well articulated the large theological commonality of Jews and Christians.

Maneuvers toward the New Testament

It has been usual to do a two-stage theological interpretation of the Old Testament, first to interpret the Old Testament "on its own terms," and then second and quite distinctly to interpret with reference to the New Testament. This procedure is evident in Brevard Childs's *Biblical Theology of the Old and New Testaments*, whereby in the second major part of the book, the Old Testament is enveloped in New Testament claims and nearly disappears.[57] Given the exclusive claims of the New Testament in its christological focus, this is perhaps the best that can be done. Any serious Old Testament interpretation, however, must be uneasy with such a procedure, precisely because it is so clear that the Old Testament does not obviously, cleanly, or directly point to Jesus or to the New Testament.

As a Christian interpreter, I think we would do better to acknowledge the independent status of the Old Testament text, and then to move toward the New Testament in something like the following maneuvers:

1. One must recognize that the Old Testament is powerfully polyphonic in its testimony, both in its substantive claims and in its characteristically elusive modes of articulation. Nothing about the theological claims of the Old Testament is obvious or one-dimensional. They remain remarkably open.

2. The polyphonic openness of the Old Testament, in substance and in modes of articulation, insists on interpretation. It is in the nature of the text to require, in each new circumstance of reading, an interpretive act that draws the text close to the

---

57   Childs, *Biblical Theology of the Old and New Testaments*, first part on pp. 95–207, second part on pp. 349–716. In Childs's presentation it is not clear how the two expositions are to be related to each other, so the problem is simply deferred.

circumstance and horizon of the interpretive community. The elusive quality of the text, moreover, invites interpretation that is free, expansive, and enormously imaginative. Thus I insist that expansive, imaginative interpretation is not an illicit abuse of the text. It is rather activity permitted and insisted on by the text.[58] This is an awareness about the text that has been vigorously resisted by positivistic historical criticism. Moreover, by identifying this quality in the text, I intend to deny the long-standing distinction between "meant" and "means," as though there is a recoverable "meant" prior to all interpretive, imaginative "means."[59] From the outset, from the ground up, the reader is engaged in giving shape to the elusiveness of the text. Historical criticism is, in fact, only one such procedure in shaping the elusive, polyphonic text in ways congruent with its circumstance, which happens to be a circumstance of positivistic rationality.

3. With the recognition that the text is polyphonic and elusive and insists on imaginative construal, it is then credible and appropriate to say that the early church, mesmerized by the person of Jesus, found it inescapable that it would draw this elusive, polyphonic text to its own circumstance, close to its experience, its memory, and its continuing sense of the transformative presence of Jesus. Thus as a confessing Christian, I believe that the imaginative construal of the Old Testament toward Jesus is a credible act and one that I fully affirm.

---

58 Such expansive interpretation is evident in the biblical text itself, as Michael Fishbane, *Biblical Interpretation in Ancient Israel* (Oxford: Clarendon Press, 1985), has shown. See, for example, Jer 3:1 as a theological redeployment of Deut 24:1–4.

59 On the distinction, see the well-known statement by Krister Stendahl, "Biblical Theology, Contemporary," *IDB* (1962), 1:418–32; see also the critical response to Stendahl by Ben C. Ollenburger, "What Krister Stendahl 'Meant'—A Normative Critique of 'Descriptive Biblical Theology,'" *HBT* 8 (June 1986) 61–98.

For purposes of Old Testament theology, however, it is important, theologically as well as historically, to insist that the connections between the two Testaments are made, as surely they must be, from the side of the New Testament and not from the side of the Old Testament. Thus it is completely appropriate to say in an act of bold, imaginative construal, as the New Testament frequently does, "The scriptures were fulfilled." Such an affirmation can be made only from the side of the fulfillment, not from the side of the Old Testament.

4. This recognition has important implications for limiting the task of Old Testament theology. It is suggested in some quarters that a Christian interpreter can only write a "biblical theology," meaning a theology of both Testaments, for the Old Testament is not available except in the presence of the New. Brevard Childs has presented a formidable example of such an enterprise. But if the Old Testament text is as polyphonic and elusive as I take it to be, then such a procedure is inherently reductionist, because it reduces the polyphonic, elusive testimony of the Old Testament to one single, exclusivist construal, namely the New Testament–christological construal, thereby violating the quality of generative openness that marks the Old Testament text. Thus my resistance to a closed model of Old Testament–New Testament is not only a practical one because I do not know enough to do it; it is also a resistance in principle.

Against such an exclusivistic linkage, I propose an alternative: that the task of Old Testament theology, as a Christian enterprise, is to articulate, explicate, mobilize, and make accessible and available the testimony of the Old Testament in all of its polyphonic, elusive, imaginative power and to offer it to the church for its continuing work of construal toward Jesus. That is, Old Testament theology, in my judgment, must prepare the material and fully respect the interpretive connections made in the New Testament and the subsequent church; but it must not make those connections, precisely because the connections are not to be found in the testimony of ancient Israel, but in the subsequent work of imaginative construal that lies beyond the text of the Old Testament. This is more than a division of labor. It is an awareness both of the *limit* of the text itself, and of the *generative power* of the text to evoke and authorize interpretations that lie beyond the scope or intention of the textual testimony as such.

The Christian imaginative construal of the Old Testament moves well beyond anything to be found in the Old Testament. The Old Testament vulnerably and willingly tolerates such use, for which it seems to present itself. The most obvious transpositions made from the ground of the Old Testament in characteristic Christian imagination include

- transposition of "messiah" to "the messiah";
- identification of the church as "the Israel of God";
- eucharistic preemption of covenant for "the new covenant";
- adversarial challenges to "the law" by an antithesis of law-grace;
- "enfleshment" of the word or spirit or wisdom in the person of Jesus.

The Old Testament text evidently permits these interpretations (but does not require them), or they would not have arisen. Old Testament theology, as a Christian enterprise, it seems to me, must resist both (a) the untenable claim that such mutations in meaning are at all *intended* by or hinted at in the Old Testament; and (b) the historical-critical, rationalistic notion that the Old Testament *precludes* such interpretive moves, for such a notion of preclusion fails to recognize the polyphonic, elusive, generative intentionality of the text.

A recognition of a permitted, but not required, imaginative construal might deliver us Christians from a two-stage interpretive process in which the second stage seems to violate the first, or from an antithesis between historical-critical and confessional-theological modes of interpretation. Better simply to recognize that these materials are deliberately evocative, and what they evoke in an interpretive practice always draws the ancient testimony into contemporaneity. The text refuses to stay past. For the church, such contemporaneity is characteristically concerned with Jesus as a historical agent, or Jesus as an undoubted and enduring power, presence, and authority in the church.

Old Testament Theology in Relation to Jewish Tradition and the Jewish Community

This theme is the counterpart to the point just expressed. That is, I have insisted that a Christian theological construal of the Old Testament is legitimate but cannot be exclusivist, as if the Old Testament pointed directly and singularly to the New Testament. Here I insist that if the church has no interpretive monopoly on the Old Testament, then it must recognize the legitimacy of other interpretive communities, of whom the primary and principal one is the Jewish community.

Old Testament theology, as a Christian enterprise, takes place in the full awareness that Judaism continues, through the centuries and generations of Christian history, to be a functioning, vibrant community of faith that has not shriveled, according to Christian dismissiveness. That community of Judaism is not consumed in Jewish legalism, according to Christian stereotype. It is not eradicated by the brutal history of Christian-sanctioned anti-Semitism. It is not, moreover, to be equated with simplistic forms of political Zionism.

I think it impossible to overstate the significance of religious Judaism for contemporary Old Testament theology, because Judaism makes unmistakably clear that this text, albeit construed in the modes of rabbinic, talmudic teaching, continues to nourish and summon a serious community of faith other than the church and alongside the church. There is no doubt, moreover, that the wonder of God's power and the majesty of God's mercy are evident in this community. This concrete, visible reality might cause Christians to lower our voices in the proclamation of exclusiveness, for it makes abundantly evident that Christian faith has no exclusive lock on the attention of the God of the Bible. Beyond voice-lowering, this recognition of Judaism might suggest that serious theological-liturgic engagement with actual Jewish communities of practice is an appropriate dimension of the practice of faithful interpretation, even with the awareness of how exceedingly difficult such engagement is.

Theological interpretation of the text is not a contextless, cerebral undertaking. It is conducted by real people who are concretely located in the historical process. That is, Old Testament theology, at the beginning of the twenty-first century, is not just an activity preoccupied with an ancient text, though it is indeed that. It is preoccupied with an ancient text in a particular circumstance. I have indicated that it was legitimate in the first century (and has been so ever since) for Christian interpretation to draw the Old Testament text to its circumstance, namely to its life with Jesus. It was legitimate, I affirm as a confessing Christian, because the text permits such evocative construal of its polyvalent quality. *Mutatis mutandis*, for us as Christians at the outset of the twenty-first century, it is legitimate and necessary to draw the Old Testament text closely to our circumstance, which is what every interpretive community inescapably does, wittingly or unwittingly.[60]

If we are to interpret the Old Testament in our circumstance, it is clear that Jewish faith and an actual Jewish community must

---

60 This is what historical criticism did in the nineteenth century in the name of objectivity, as it embraced developmentalism in the context of great cultural developmentalist undertakings.

be on the horizon of Christians. More specifically, Old Testament theology as a Christian enterprise must be done in light (or darkness!) of the Holocaust and the unthinkable brutality wrought against the Jewish community in a society with Christian roots.[61] I do not flinch from the acknowledgment that our particular post-Holocaust situation of interpretation imposes on us important interpretive requirements, even if attentiveness to Jewishness were not integral to the text itself.[62]

Christian interpretation of the Old Testament and its characteristic supersessionism stand a long distance removed from the Holocaust. Yet the thinking behind and around supersessionism, of which Christian Old Testament theology has been one aspect, is indeed linked to the Holocaust. Therefore Christian Old Testament theology, at the end of the twentieth century, must make important and generous adjustments in our conventional and uncritical exclusivist claims on the Old Testament. That is, what is theologically required *by the text* as such is positively reinforced *by historical circumstance* and its enduring demands.

If Christian appropriation of the Old Testament toward Jesus is an act of claiming the elusive tradition toward a Jesus-circumstance, we can recognize that other imaginative appropriations of this elusive tradition are equally legitimate and appropriate. We have yet to

---

61 On the cruciality of the Holocaust for the future of both Jewish and Christian theology, see especially Emil Fackenheim, *To Mend the World: Foundations of Post-Holocaust Thought* (2d ed.; New York: Schocken Books, 1989); and *The Jewish Bible after the Holocaust: A Rereading* (Bloomington: Indiana University Press, 1990).

62 The Holocaust is unique, even when we recognize that it serves paradigmatically to call attention to other programmatic abuses of the vulnerable. Thus my comments on the issue of Jewishness in Old Testament theology are intrinsically connected to my comments on justice in Old Testament theology. The Holocaust is the quintessential betrayal of justice, which is why it continues to evoke such a rich and troubled theological response.

decide how christological exclusiveness is to be articulated so that it is not an ideological ground for the dismissal of a co-community of interpretation.[63] Thus our most passionate affirmation of Jesus as the "clue" to all of reality must allow for other "clues" found herein by other serious communities of interpretation. And of course this applies to none other so directly as it does to Judaism.

Thus Christians are able to say of the Old Testament, "It is ours," but must also say, "It is not ours alone." This means to recognize that Jewish imaginative construals of the Old Testament text are, in Christian purview, a legitimate theological activity. More than that, Jewish imaginative construal of the text is a legitimate theological activity to which Christians must pay attention. I have no doubt that Christian supersessionism, enforced as it is by the classical modes of Hellenistic thought, has made it nearly impossible for Christians to attend to the riches of Judaism. Once we recognize that theological construal and imagination other than our own is legitimate, however, we may take it into serious account. I do not imagine that attention to this primal alternative construal of the text will lead to an abrupt overthrow of distinctive Christian claims. But I also do not imagine that such attention would leave Christian claims untouched, certainly not untouched in their fearful, destructive aspects, but perhaps also not untouched in good-faith exclusivism, rooted in a text that remains as elusive as its Subject and that relentlessly resists closure.

Old Testament Theology and the Problem of Justice

Whatever one may think of Israel's historical antecedents and Yahwism's religious antecedents (and there were plenty of both), it is

---

63 Among Christian theologians, Jürgen Moltmann, *The Way of Jesus Christ: Christology in Messianic Dimensions* (1990; Minneapolis: Fortress Press, 1993), has given particular care precisely to this issue.

clear that in something like "the Mosaic revolution" Yahweh burst into world history as a theological *novum*. This Mosaic revolution has political, economic, moral, and ethnic connotations, but its main force, I suggest, is to establish justice as the core focus of Yahweh's life in the world and Israel's life with Yahweh.

The Mosaic revolution, which is the principal focus of the Pentateuch (and which in turn is the principal reference point of Israel's subsequent tradition), has two points of accent: as event and as institution. The event that forms the center of Israel's liturgic imagination is the Exodus. The Exodus, as it has been stylized in Israel's liturgic texts, is for the glorification of Yahweh (cf. Exod 14:4, 17). But that glorification of Yahweh was possible only through the emancipation of the Hebrew slaves from the oppressiveness of Egyptian bondage (Exod 14:14, 25; see also Ezek 36:22–32; 39:25–29). From the outset, Yahweh is known to be a God committed to the establishment of concrete, sociopolitical justice in a world of massive power organized against justice.

In that event, as given us in Israel's core testimony, Yahweh's profound resolve toward the reordering of social power is voiced in the initial imperative addressed to Pharaoh: "Let my people go" (Exod 5:1). Behind that resolve, which is then relentlessly implemented in the plague narrative, is the voiced suffering of the slaves (Exod 2:23) that becomes the driving power of Yahweh's alternative history (Exod 2:23–25; 3:7–10). It is voiced suffering that sets in motion Yahweh's uncompromising resolve for the transformation of earthly power arrangements.

The second accent of the Mosaic revolution is the Sinai proclamation of Yahweh's commandments, which seeks to give stable, institutional form to the social possibilities engendered in the Exodus. Thus the commandments appeal to Yahweh's iconoclastic inclination (Exod 20:4–7) and from that inclination enunciate an alternative social possibility in the world.

It is fair to say that given its subsequent exposition through time, the Exodus event and the Sinai structure do indeed witness to Yahweh's preferential option for the poor, weak, and marginated.[64] Or said another way, Yahweh is here known to be a resilient and relentless advocate of and agent for justice, which entails the complete reordering of power arrangements in the earth.

In the context of Israel's completed testimony, it is difficult to overstate the pivotal importance for the rest of Israel's testimony of the Mosaic revolution and the commitment of Yahweh (and of Israel) to justice. If we consider in turn the prophetic, psalmic, sapiential, and apocalyptic texts, it seems evident that Israel, everywhere and without exhaustion, is preoccupied with the agenda of justice that is rooted in the character and resolve of Yahweh. This justice rooted in Yahweh, moreover, is to be enacted and implemented concretely in human practice.

It is important that we recognize with some precision the quality and intention of Mosaic, Yahwistic justice, for it is easily misunderstood, given the easy and careless use of the term *justice*. The intention of Mosaic justice is to redistribute social goods and social power; thus it is distributive justice.[65] This justice recognizes that social goods and social power are unequally and destructively

---

64 The Exodus event and the Sinai structure are of course particularly and peculiarly Jewish. They are, at the same time, paradigmatic for every marginated human community. See Jon Levenson, "Exodus and Liberation," *The Hebrew Bible, the Old Testament, and Historical Criticism*, 127–59; and Walter Brueggemann, "Pharaoh as Vassal: A Study of a Political Metaphor," *CBQ* 57 (1995) 27–51.

65 The most articulate presentation of distributive justice in the Old Testament known to me is by José Miranda, *Marx and the Bible: A Critique of the Philosophy of Oppression* (Maryknoll, N.Y.: Orbis Books, 1974) 77–108 and passim. See also Rolf P. Knierim, *The Task of Old Testament Theology* (Grand Rapids: Eerdmans, 1995) 86–122, and Moshe Weinfeld, *Social Justice in Ancient Israel and in the Ancient Near East* (Minneapolis: Fortress Press, 1995).

distributed in Israel's world (and derivatively in any social context), and that the well-being of the community requires that social goods and power to some extent be given up by those who have too much, for the sake of those who have not enough.

This enormously radical principle is constitutive for revolutionary Israel and for Yahweh, as is evidenced in various traditions.[66] We may cite three specific cases that witness to this distributive intention.

1. In Exodus (3:21–22; 11:2; and 12:35–36) the Israelites are urged by Moses to take "jewelry of silver and gold" from the Egyptians when they depart slavery. This remembered action perhaps is nothing more than the resentful seizure of the "have-nots" from the "haves," but that it occupies so prominent a place in the narrative texts suggests that it constitutes something of a principle of redeployment. Moreover, David Daube has proposed that this act is related to the "law of release" in Deut 15:1–11, wherein the released bond servant is entitled to economic viability.[67]

2. The narrative of manna, a sign of Yahweh's protective generosity toward Israel, is a model of alternative management of food supplies. As the manna is given and gathered, it is reported: ". . . those who gathered much had nothing over, and those who gathered little had no shortage; they gathered as much as each of them needed" (Exod 16:18; cf. 2 Cor 8:15). This statement

---

66 Norman Gottwald has been vigorously criticized for his use of the term *egalitarian* with reference to the Sinai revolution. More recently, he has articulated his sense of the revolutionary dimension of Mosaism by the use of the term *communitarian*; *The Hebrew Bible in Its Social World and Ours* (Atlanta: Scholars Press, 1993) xxv–xxvii.

67 David Daube, *The Exodus Pattern in the Bible* (London: Faber and Faber, 1963) 55–61. On this text, see also Jeffries M. Hamilton, *Social Justice and Deuteronomy: The Case of Deuteronomy 15* (SBLDS; Atlanta: Scholars Press, 1992).

is no doubt intended as a model for how a community should mobilize its resources for the benefit of all.

3. The legal corpus of Deuteronomy is preoccupied with "widows, orphans, and aliens," those who lack resources and who lack social leverage to secure resources.[68] The Mosaic revolution, broadly construed, intends that the powerful are under obligation to practice distributive justice.

The reason we should pay careful attention to the substance of distributive justice is that the term *justice*, which in many texts of Israel requires reparations, more conventionally in our society means retributive justice: giving to persons what is their just deserts on the basis of performance; that is, a system of rewards and punishments, not informed by the communal obligation or the generosity of the community. No doubt the practice of retributive justice has a presence in the Old Testament, as it does in the religious environment of the ancient world.[69] There is no doubt, moreover, that the term *justice*, as used in the contemporary world, usually refers to retributive justice, as in the widespread zeal for "law and order."

Both *distributive* justice and *retributive* justice can find warrant in the text of Israel. It seems unambiguous, however, that in Israel's core texts related to the Mosaic revolution, Yahwism is a practice of *distributive* justice. If that is the case, interpreters of the Old Testament must always be precise in their articulation, or they are sure to

---

68 Moshe Weinfeld, "Humanism," *Deuteronomy and the Deuteronomic School* (Oxford: Clarendon Press, 1972) 282–97, refers to this agenda in the Book of Deuteronomy as "humanistic."

69 See Exod 21:23; Deut 19:21. More generally, the Book of Proverbs inclines in this direction. See Norman Whybray, *Wealth and Poverty in the Book of Proverbs* (JSOTSup 99; Sheffield: Sheffield Academic Press, 1990); and J. David Pleins, "Poverty in the Social World of the Wise," *JSOT* 37 (1987) 61–78.

be misheard in terms of a justice that is less costly and less demanding on those with a disproportion of power and goods.[70]

It is important not to romanticize the commitment of Yahwism to distributive justice, even though it stands at the core of Israel's testimony about Yahweh. In the Old Testament, not everyone everywhere is an enthusiast for distributive justice. Distributive justice, if taken seriously (as in the practice of Jubilee), is inherently destabilizing of the status quo, for redistribution means to place established interests in jeopardy. Thus it does not surprise us that the benefactors of the status quo—those who are advantaged by present political, economic, and legal arrangements—believe that the maintenance of "order"—that is, the present order—is a primary function of Yahweh. It is likely that this social interest is reflected in the sapiential traditions of Proverbs that seem to urge generosity, but not structural change or serious redistribution.[71] And it seems plausible to understand the familiar strictures of the early prophets against self-indulgence to be in dispute with royal traditions, which seem to justify accumulations of surplus value. Israelite society, like every society, was deeply vexed in the ongoing tension between "haves" and "have-nots" who become, respectively, advocates (in the name of Yahweh) of social equilibrium and social transformation.

A study of Old Testament theology must recognize, with social realism, that both advocates of distributive justice and of order are present and vocal in the community, and both claim the support of Yahweh in their theological testimony. At the minimum, it is important to recognize and explicate this tension. In my judgment, however, one may go further to insist that while both sorts

---

70 See Miranda, *Marx and the Bible*, on Jer 22:15–16 for a most radical statement on the matter.

71 See Robert Gordis, "The Social Background of Wisdom Literature," *Poets, Prophets, and Sages: Essays in Biblical Interpretation* (Bloomington: Indiana University Press, 1971) 160–97.

of advocates bear testimony to Yahweh, there can be little doubt that the adherents of distributive justice occupy the central space in the theological testimony of Israel, so that in canonical Yahwism, distributive justice is indeed a primary urging.

Having acknowledged that both justice and order are present as theological claims in the text, we may suggest that in rough outline, there is a general commitment in Israel's testimony to justice as a primary agenda of Yahweh. This is a somewhat reductionist or thematized judgment on my part. It is important to make it, however, in order to observe that when Israelite tradition is placed in juxtaposition to the great classical traditions of Hellenistic philosophy, justice is clearly a Jewish, Yahwistic preoccupation, whereas the Greeks endlessly focus on order.[72] Indeed, nothing in the Greek tradition approximates a Yahwistic passion for distributive justice, which anticipates that the present social order stands under criticism and in jeopardy, in the interest of a promised and coming just order that benefits all members of the community. Thus appeals to order in the royal, sapiential texts of Israel must not be overstated, for when contrasted with the Greeks, the Israelite tradition is as odd as it is insistent on this point.

Thus there is something revolutionary, transformative, and subversive about Israel's testimony.[73] No doubt, as Norman Gottwald has indicated, much of this tendency is sociologically driven.[74] But as Gottwald also recognizes, the sociological has a theological counterpoint, and Israel does not flinch, in the end, from locating

---

72 Northrop Frye, *The Critical Path: An Essay on the Social Context of Literary Criticism* (Bloomington: Indiana University Press, 1971) 334–55, comments on the contrast between a general "myth of concern" and a more concrete "myth of freedom" that has its roots in the Bible.

73 On the revolutionary generativity of Israel's testimony, see Michael Walzer, *Exodus and Revolution* (New York: Basic Books, 1986).

74 Gottwald, *The Tribes of Yahweh: A Sociology of the Religion of Liberated Israel, 1250–1050 B.C.E.* (London: SCM Press, 1980) 608–18.

the base of its passion for revolutionary justice in the character of Yahweh.[75]

Having said that justice for Israel is rooted in the very character of Yahweh, we may go on to notice a peculiar note in Israel's candor about Yahweh. In its narratives and hymns celebrating Yahweh's justice, Yahweh is said to be a "lover of justice" (cf. Ps 99:4; Isa 61:8).[76] That much is not in dispute, and Israel counts heavily on it. But Israel is realistic and candid about its life situation. It knows very well that life is not as just as it might be if Yahweh's passionate, sovereign will for justice were enacted. It is this realism and candor that evoke in Israel what has come to be called theodicy.

We must, however, be quite clear on what this theme entails in Israel. In the philosophical tradition of theodicy since Gottfried Wilhelm Leibniz, theodicy has been understood as an explanatory enterprise: to "justify the ways of God to man." In Israel, however, what is called theodicy is not explanation but protest.[77] Acknowledging that the world is unjust, Israel has no interest in justifying an unjust world in making excuses for Yahweh, or in protecting Yahweh from criticism for failure to right the world. Rather, Israel characteristically presents itself, in "theodic" texts, as the great advocate and champion of justice, on which Yahweh has reneged. Thus in the most obvious texts of Jer 12:1–3 and Job 21:7, Israel voices its vexation toward Yahweh. In the psalms of complaint and in the larger poem of Job, moreover, Yahweh is under assault for not in fact practicing the justice to which Yahweh is ostensibly committed by covenant oath.[78]

---

75   Ibid., 618–21. See James L. Mays, "Justice: Perspectives from the Prophetic Tradition," *Int* 37 (1983) 5–17.

76   On the peculiar piety of the poor, see Norbert Lohfink, *Lobgesange der Armen: Studien zum Magnifikat, den Hodajot von Qumran und einigen späten Psalmen* (Stuttgart: Verlag Katholisches Bibelwerk, 1990).

77   On theodicy, see the collection of essays in James L. Crenshaw, ed., *Theodicy in the Old Testament* (IRT 4; Philadelphia: Fortress Press, 1983).

78   Most radically Job 9:15–22.

In its deepest vexation, then, Israel makes a distinction between Yahweh and the reality of justice. While we might expect that Yahweh is ultimate and justice penultimate, in some of Israel's most desperate utterances, matters are inverted. Justice is held up as ultimate, and Yahweh as an agent of justice is critiqued for failure of justice. That is, Israel is aware that there is more to Yahweh than justice: there is holiness and downright capricious irascibility. Sometimes Israel is awed and deferential before this staggering ultimacy of Yahweh. In its texts of protest, however, Israel has no time for or interest in Yahweh's wild, unresponsive quality. In those texts, Israel would seem to value justice more than Yahweh. This is not because Israel is legalistic, or because Israel prefers a set of principles to a live agent. On the contrary, it is because Israel is irreducibly committed to material, concrete well-being, and not even Yahweh's own character will talk Israel out of its passion for well-being in the earth. Thus Yahweh in heaven must "get with the program" of *shalôm* on earth!

This curious inversion is oddly and wondrously voiced by Jacques Derrida. Derrida is known primarily as the progenitor of deconstruction, a program in which nothing is finally absolute enough to escape critique. It is clear, however, that Derrida's deconstruction is indeed a form of Jewish iconoclasm.[79] It is for that reason that Derrida, in the face of his passion for deconstruction, can finally write of "the indeconstructability of justice."[80] This is not only a mouthful (and especially a mouthful for Derrida), it is a characteristically Jewish mouthful. In this phrasing, Derrida

---

79 See my discussion of the links between deconstruction and Jewish iconoclasm, pp. 329–32.

80 Jacques Derrida, "Force of Law: The 'Mythical Foundation of Authority,'" *Cardozo Law Review* 11 (1990) 919–1045. I have not had access to the article by Derrida, but refer to it from the citation of John D. Caputo, *Demythologizing Heidegger* (Bloomington: Indiana University Press, 1993) 193.

is appealing back to the center of the Mosaic revolution, to what is finally and normatively the case with Yahweh. There are, to be sure, many compromises of this claim in the interest of established social interest in the testimony of the Old Testament. At the same time, there is no doubt that none of these compromises or uneasinesses touches the main claim made about Yahweh and about the future of the earth.[81] In the tradition of Job (and of Derrida), I suggest, Yahweh is held to justice, and if Yahweh cannot subscribe to this earthly passion, then the claims of heaven must be deconstructed.

Theological interpreters of the Old Testament at the end of the twentieth century must, in my judgment, pay primal attention to this irreducible claim of justice, which is, in the most abrasive parts of the testimony, a demanding summons even to Yahweh. This passion for justice stands as a revolutionary, subversive challenge to Jews and to Christians, and to every alternative metanarrative. Specifically, I suggest, at the end of the twentieth century Israel's testimony about Yahweh stands as a profound challenge to the dominant metanarrative of technological, military consumerism. The claim that capitalist ideology has irrevocably defeated every rival, a claim brazenly articulated by Francis Fukuyama, is the context in which Old Testament theology must now be undertaken.[82]

The apparent defeat of Marxist ideology and the incredible concentration of power in the market economies of the United States and Japan indicate a drastic reordering of social relationships in the

---

81 I refer to the readiness of Israel's testimony to proceed in an uncritical way on patriarchal assumptions. I have no wish to deny that the text is pervasively committed to such assumptions. Rather than to dismiss the text on these grounds, however, I count on Israel's characteristic propensity to mount a serious, shrill protest and summons to Yahweh (and to Yahweh's text) to new accountability.

82 Francis Fukuyama, *The End of History and the Last Man* (New York: Free Press, 1992).

twenty-first century. I have termed the driving power of this new economic wealth "technological, military consumerism." I would not quibble about the phrasing, but I mean by this phrase that: (a) consumerism is the conviction that the unit of social meaning is the detached individual whose self and identity consist in consumption; (b) such unbridled consumption requires a disproportion of wealth and advantage, which must be defended by military means (for example, immigration policy); and (c) this defense of advantage is readily and simply justified by a one-dimensional technological mind-set that in principle brackets out of consideration all human questions. There can be little doubt of the pragmatic power of this ideology, however it be named or stylized in specifics.

This ideology is indeed totalizing, so that every aspect of the life of every one of us is impinged on and to some extent constrained by it. It is evident that this totalizing ideology has enormous power. It is equally evident, I take it, that this ideology is in the end deathly, so that it robs us of our humanness as it robs, at the same time, our environment of creation of a chance for life. I have no desire to exaggerate the case in theatrical terms, though it seems to me well-nigh impossible to overstate the case.

While the above comments may seem odd in an Old Testament theology, I have not strayed from my topic. Israel's testimony, with its uncompromising and irreducible commitment to justice, stands as the primary alternative to the deathly ideology of technological, military consumerism. In a variety of ways, in an endless variety of textual utterances, Israel's testimony is to the effect that Yahweh's passion for justice, passion for the well-being of the human community, and passion for the *shalôm* of the earth will refuse to come to terms with the power of death, no matter its particular public form or its ideological garb.[83]

---

83 On the aggressive power of death as it threatens the lifeworld offered by Yahweh, see Jon Levenson, *Creation and the Persistence of Evil:*

It is possible to transpose the testimony of Israel about Yahweh, so that the issue with alternative metanarratives is never joined, or so that Yahweh is made to be so anemic that there can be no conflict. The transposition of this testimony into an innocuous text can take place in many ways, such as the distancing effect of critical study that recognizes everything except the main claims, or scholastic theology that turns elusive testimony into closed system, or what I call "horizontal liberalism," in which the agency of Yahweh evaporates into social ideology.

If Old Testament theology is worth doing in time to come, it will be required to focus on primary theological claims. The focus on these main claims will not be a mere interesting theological exploration, but a life-and-death struggle for the future of the world. After all, Israel's articulation of this testimony was not innocuous. It sought to convince "the court" that this construal of reality was true, over against false alternatives. That work of convincing is not finished. As in any court where capital punishment is the option,[84] true testimony becomes a life-and-death matter.

The Jewish Drama of Divine Omnipotence (San Francisco: Harper and Row, 1988); and Fredrik Lindström, Suffering and Sin: Interpretations of Illness in the Individual Complaint Psalms (Stockholm: Almqvist and Wiksell International, 1994).

84 I use the term capital punishment in order to refer not only literally to its practice, but also metaphorically to the "execution" of the entire creation.

MOVING TOWARD TRUE SPEECH

Old Testament theology in the future, I have proposed, will be a reflection on Israel's disclosing speech that is in a pluralistic context and therefore inescapably disputatious. It is my sense that a community of interpretation that engages in a serious undertaking of Old Testament theology will itself be a community that attends to disclosing speech in a pluralistic context that is inescapably disputatious. I mean by this that Old Testament theology is not simply a detached *analysis* of an ancient practice of speech, but it is *an engagement with* those speech practices, in order to adjudicate what is and what is not "true speech," that is, speech about the truth.

It follows that an engagement that is such a dispute about true speech both evokes and requires a certain kind of community—a community with an intentional speech practice of its own. There must be a place and a group of people, over time and through time and in time, who engage in such a practice. Therefore a community intent on Old Testament theology must have a certain form of life to it, a life that is prepared to acknowledge the rootedness, richness, and density of the practice it undertakes.

By insisting that Old Testament theology requires a certain form of life, I am, in the end, accepting that Old Testament theology is an enterprise that belongs properly to an ecclesial community, a community that is unembarrassed about commitment that, in the parlance of "objective rationality," may be categorized as bias or ideology. (I do not intend to make any assumption that such an ecclesial community must be in official, traditional, recognized, institutional forms, but only that it should be intent on dangerous life in the presence of the God attested in this testimony.)

I suggest that we acknowledge, more forthrightly than has been the case, *a division of labor between the academic and ecclesial interpreting communities.* The academy, for historical reasons of self-understanding, is in the modern world committed to a rationality that precludes the density of commitment and passion that I believe necessarily pertains to serious Old Testament theology.[85] By such a statement I do not concede that the academy is "objective" or "neutral" or "scientific," for its commitments are as visible and demanding and exclusionary as those of any ecclesial community. They are, however, very different, and therefore in its practice of its rationality it is likely that the academy will never move seriously beyond "history of religion." For myself, I believe that is an acceptable, legitimate, and needed undertaking.

The other side of the matter is to recognize that such an undertaking, given its epistemological stance, is never likely to engage the serious theological claims of the text with an intensity commensurate to the intensity of the claims in the text. Such full engagement would require a community of interpretation that is as unrestrained (neither held in discipline nor blinded and disabled, depending on one's view) as is the academy, but is free to host the truth of the testimony given here. Such a division of labor requires, in my judgment, that both enterprises, academic and ecclesial, are recognized as legitimate, that both are engaged in something important and indispensable to full understanding, and that both communities must pay attention to the work of the other. That is, Old Testament theology, as it may be conducted in ecclesial communities, is not

---

85 There are, to be sure, important exceptions to this statement; e.g., the great group of German expositors who grew out of the Confessing Church and who produced the poignant commentaries in the Biblischer Kommentar series. I am speaking of the characteristic epistemological situation of the academy in the United States. See the discussion of Robert A. Segal, *Explaining and Interpreting Religion: Essays on the Issues* (Toronto Studies in Religion 16; New York: Peter Lang, 1992). Segal's appeal to the distinction between explanation and interpretation is telling about his assumptions. Notice that on p. 122, he speaks of the "fear" "religionists" have of social scientific explanations of religion. This seems to me a peculiarly self-serving judgment.

in principle a second-rate or secondhand enterprise, but it can be a serious intellectual and moral undertaking that is not enthralled to a Cartesian attempt to think without body. It is my view that the academic community (of which I am gladly a part), except for the most extreme and most irresponsible cases, can respect and take seriously such ecclesial exposition, when it is well done and when it is congruent with the actual practice of the community. To refuse to learn from such ecclesial scholarship because it is not "scientific" enough strikes me as irresponsible and obscurantist.

Such ecclesial theological interpretation, however, must be responsibly done, making use of the best learning available and engaging in practice commensurate with its interpretation. That is, in the end, theological interpretation that engages the theological claims of the text must host the testimony in all its oddness, and must be engaged in the practice of the core testimony and counter-testimony, in practice and in obedience, in protest and complaint, with its whole life. The phrase "engaged in practice" means for me not only hearing the text, but living intentionally in response to its proposed world. Here I briefly reiterate two sorts of arguments I have already made, this time with an eye on practical implementation in contemporary life.

Four Enduring Issues

Ecclesial communities of interpretation that attend in serious ways to this text may focus intentionally on what I have identified as four enduring issues intrinsic to Old Testament theology:[86]

1. Attendance to a form of *criticism* of the text that is congruent with our intellectual circumstance of pluralism, which reck-ons with the density and elusiveness of the text.

---

86 For my discussion of these four issues, see pp. 102–14 and chap. 28.

2. Self-conscious mobilization of the Old Testament text *toward the New Testament*, but with full awareness that the text so construed is open, polyphonic, elusive, and imaginative, beyond any single rendering, including that of the church.

3. Attendance to the *Jewish community* as co-reader, co-hearer, and co-practitioner of this text, whereby the community that Christians have long demonized becomes a heeded truth-teller.

4. Awareness that at the core of this construed world is a claim of *distributive justice* that is concrete, material, revolutionary, subversive, and uncompromising.

Form of Life for Community of Interpretation

Concrete practice as a "form of life" may be guided and informed by what I have marked as the "form of life" this testimony necessarily has taken in the practice of ancient Israel.[87] Thus an ecclesial community of interpretation may:

1. Dwell in the tradition of *Torah*, accepting the narratives and the commands of purity and of debt cancellation as the principal sources of funding for obedient imagination.

2. Engage, after the manner of *royal agency*, in the practice of power for well-being, a practice of power that is always a temptation and always under criticism.

3. Host the disruptive *prophetic voices*, which concern the costs and pains of the historical process, and the possibilities that well up in the midst of the costs and pains.

4. Practice, after the manner of *the Priestly traditions*, the presence of Yahweh, which embraces the sacramental freightedness of all of life.

---

87 For my discussion of the five elements of Israel's "form of life" to which I have alluded, see chaps. 20–24.

5. Know, in an embrace of the *traditions of wisdom*, the dailiness of life in all of its contested, buoyant density.

Such a community, when it proceeds with intentionality, draws the text and its testimony close to its own life. But it also moves its own life under the assurances and demands of a text that continues in its odd, inscrutable, nonnegotiable otherness.

The Idiom of Israel's Faith

I am helped by a recent phrase of Christopher Bollas, who, in his reflection on personality theory, has transposed Freud's id as the most elemental dimension of self into "idiom."[88] Bollas suggests that health, well-being, and maturity depend on identifying, embracing, and practicing the peculiar, distinctive idiom of life with which one is born. *Mutatis mutandis*, I suggest that responsible Old Testament theology in an ecclesial community of interpretation is interpretation done in an idiom that is congruent with the life setting of the community, but that is drawn from, informed by, and authorized by the idiom of the testimony of the text. For all its variation through time and in different circumstances, there is a recognizable idiom to Israel's testimony, especially as some texts take great liberties with it.[89] That idiom is the one we have identified in the core testimony,

---

88 Christopher Bollas, *Being a Character: Psychoanalysis and Self Experience* (London: Routledge, 1993) 17, 64–65, 70–71. Bollas considers the psychic process as one of deconstructing and then constructing a new "form of existence."

89 The extreme cases are the Song of Solomon and Ecclesiastes. The canonizing and interpretive processes no doubt have drawn these texts into the orbit of Israel's more characteristic testimony, so that in canonical location and form one may perhaps hear echoes of standard Israelite cadences. Admittedly this requires some stretch of hearing, but that is what Israel characteristically undertakes, though the push to consensus must not be overstated.

made fuller and richer by the countertestimony that is evoked in response against the core testimony and its power. The combination of core testimony and countertestimony constitutes the idiom of Israel's faith. It is, then, this idiom that may be practiced in an ecclesial community of interpretation.

In contemporary ecclesial communities of theological interpretation, that ancient idiom is recoverable when the community accepts that its own cadences and dialect are derivative from that idiom. That is, such a community of interpretation moves past the Cartesian dilemma—now aware of the great suspicions of Freud and Marx, fully present to the great ruptures of Auschwitz and Hiroshima—to a buoyant "second naiveté," in the end convinced that no cadence of speech, no dialect of communication, no idiom of self-discernment is as powerful, as compelling, as liberating, or as transformative as this one, whereby one may speak and live unencumbered in a world of threat.[90]

In the end, my appeal to ecclesial communities, and especially to their leaders and pastors, is that there be a serious reengagement with this idiom, which is the *Muttersprach* of the church (as of the synagogue).[91] It is my impression that the church in the West has been sorely tempted to speak in everyone's idiom except its own. Liberals, embarrassed by the otherness of the biblical idiom, have kept control of matters through rationalistic speech that in

---

90   On the rupture of the Holocaust as it bears on theological work, see the citations for Emil Fackenheim in chap. 28, n. 20; and Richard L. Rubenstein, *After Auschwitz: History, Theology, and Contemporary Judaism* (2d ed.; Baltimore: Johns Hopkins University Press, 1992). On the second naiveté, see above chap. 2, n. 81.

91   Reference might usefully be made to John Murray Cuddihy, *The Ordeal of Civility: Freud, Marx, Levi-Strauss and the Jewish Struggle with Modernity* (New York: Basic Books, 1974), for it is modernity that has required Jews to squelch their *Muttersprach*. See Cynthia Ozick, "Toward a New Yiddish," *Art and Ardor: Essays* (New York: Alfred A. Knopf, 1983) 151–77.

the end affirms that "God has no hands but ours," issuing in burdensome self-congratulations. Conservatives, fearful of speech that is undomesticated, have insisted on flattening biblical testimony into the settled categories of scholasticism that freezes truth.[92] In both sorts of speech, the incommensurate, mutual One disappears. Neither liberal rationalism nor scholastic conservatism will yield any energy or freedom for serious, sustained obedience or for buoyant elemental trust. Old Testament theology is, in an ecclesial setting, an activity for the recovery of an idiom of speech and of life that is congruent with the stuff of Israel's faith. Where that idiom is engaged and practiced, openings may appear in the shut-down world of contemporaneity, openings for core testimony revisited and for countertestimony reuttered.

Acknowledgment of Yahweh Requires Reordering of Everything Else

I conclude this exposition with two references to the cruciality of testimony in the life and identity of Israel, the people of this text. The testimony of Israel concerning Yahweh is always of two kinds, one to reorder *the internal life* of the community in ways faithful to Yahweh, the other to invite *the world out beyond* this community to reorder its life with reference to Yahweh. Both enterprises are preoccupied with the recognition that the acknowledgment of Yahweh at the center of life (the life of Israel or the life of the world) requires a reordering of everything else. Both texts I will cite advocate a particular construal of reality but are finally aware that alternative, competing construals of reality are available and might

---

92 It will be evident that in my own practice of a cultural-linguistic perspective, my opposition is to perspectives and approaches that George A. Lindbeck, *The Nature of Doctrine: Religion and Theology in a Postliberal Age* (London: SPCK, 1984), has termed, respectively, "expressive-experiential" and "propositional."

be chosen. The recognition of a viable alternative to the world of Yahweh adds to the sense of urgency in the text.

The first text, in Joshua 24, is of peculiar importance in recent scholarship. In this text Joshua, successor to Moses, gathers together the traditions of the Torah (vv. 2–13) and invites the assembly to make a decision for or against the God of this recital—and consequently, for or against the alternative gods "beyond the River and in Egypt" (vv. 14–15).[93] The meeting at Shechem is one of serious, even dangerous adjudication, in order to decide the truth of competing gods, based on competing testimonies. At the outset the assembly is prepared to serve Yahweh, to attest to the truth and reliability of the Yahweh-story (vv. 16–18). Joshua, however, as a loyal adherent to rigorous Mosaism, does not make an embrace of Yahweh an easy one, for Yahweh is a harsh, demanding, uncompromising God:

> You cannot serve the Lord, for he is a holy God. He is a jealous God; he will not forgive your transgressions or your sins. If you forsake the Lord and serve foreign gods, then he will turn and do you harm, and consume you, after having done you good. (vv. 19–20)

The community is not deterred by Joshua's warning and persists in its resolve to embrace Yahweh (v. 21).

Having tested their resolve, Joshua responds with a harsh and onerous warning:

> "You are witnesses against yourselves that you have chosen the Lord, to serve him." And they said, "We are witnesses." (v. 22)

---

93 On this text and its praxis, see Walter Brueggemann, *Biblical Perspectives on Evangelism: Living in a Three-Storied Universe* (Nashville: Abingdon Press, 1993) 48–70.

I cite this exchange as evidence that Israel's role as witness is a heavy one. Israel takes a solemn oath and substantiates it in a most solemn way. Israel has been warned and is fully informed about the rigors of a life with Yahweh. Israel's first testimony is that it has engaged with Yahweh willingly, knowingly, and without reservation. This act of testimony, moreover, requires a purging of all competing loyalties and a resolve for obedience (v. 23). Testimony is not easy talk; it is rather an elemental decision to reorder the life of the community with an entirely different set of risks and possibilities. This community, set in motion that day at Shechem by Joshua, continues wherever this decision for loyalty is undertaken. Israel's decision for loyalty to Yahweh is in the presence and awareness of alternative loyalties, here vigorously and intentionally rejected.

The second text I cite is Isa 43:8–13. This text is as disputatious as the one in Joshua 24, only in a different arena. The text in Joshua 24 concerned the internal ordering of Israel's life vis-à-vis competing religious alternatives. In Isaiah 43 the scope of concern is larger, for now the contested issue concerns Yahweh versus the gods of Babylon and a decision about the truth of world governance. This text in Isaiah 43 is articulated in a mode of advocacy, and it has been rightly recognized by Claus Westermann as a "trial speech."[94]

The subject of the disputation concerns "the true God," whether Yahweh or the gods of the empire. The argument about "true God," however, turns on the effectiveness of competing witnesses. Claus Westermann comments:

> The figure he uses, that of a legal process, is intended to suggest that the present hour in history is the time for the final decision of the claim of divinity as between the God of

---

94 Claus Westermann, *Isaiah 40–66: A Commentary* (OTL; Philadelphia: Westminster Press, 1969) 120–26. On p. 119, Westermann speaks of "trial speech."

Israel on one side and *all* the gods of all the nations on the other. . . . In this legal process, the evidence under consideration consists of objective facts, which both sides must accept. If therefore the gods do bring such evidence, then the other side, too—that is, Yahweh and Israel—are bound to listen to it and allow that it is true. What a daring thing to say! Everything staked on one throw! . . . This, however, requires witnesses to testify to it, that is, those who confess the divinity of the god in question.[95]

The oracle of Isa 43:8–9 begins with a taunting invitation by Yahweh to the witnesses for the alternative gods, witnesses who are taken to be blind, deaf, and ineffectual.[96] That is, the allegedly pitiful quality of the gods is, in this imaginative scenario, expressed in terms of the disability of the witnesses:

> *Bring forth the people who are blind, yet have eyes, who*
> *   are deaf, yet have ears!*
> *Let all the nations gather together,*
> *and let the peoples assemble.*
> *Who among them declared this,*
> *and foretold to us the former things? (Isa 43:8–9)*

The poem abruptly changes course with "You" at the beginning of v. 10, now addressing Israel. In the address to Israel, two matters are skillfully interwoven. One is a repeated insistence on Yahweh as the only God, who created and formed and saved, besides whom there is no other god, no alien god. Second

---

95 Ibid., 121–22.
96 With the scholarly consensus, Westermann regards the blind and deaf witnesses as Yahweh's witnesses. Against that view, I take them to be witnesses for the other, dysfunctional gods. The point, however, is not important to my argument.

is a reiterated statement, "You are my witnesses," who are to attest to these singular, lyrical claims:

> *You are my witnesses, says the Lord,*
> *and my servant whom I have chosen,*
> *so that you may know and believe me*
> *and understand that I am he.*
> *Before me no god was formed,*
> *nor shall there be any after me.*
> *I, I am the Lord,*
> *and besides me there is no savior.*
> *I declared and saved and proclaimed,*
> *when there was no strange god among you;*
> *and you are my witnesses, says the Lord.*
> *I am God, and also henceforth I am He;*
> *there is no one who can deliver from my hand;*
> *I work and who can hinder it? (vv. 10–13)*

Yahweh has taken the initiative in choosing the witnesses so that they may know and believe in Yahweh; and because they know and believe, they can and must testify.

What concerns us is the intimate connection between the role of the witnesses and the singular theological claims of Yahweh. It is clear that in the drama of the courtroom, the claim of Yahweh depends on the word of the witnesses.

In Isa 44:8 the same linkage is evident.[97] "There is no other rock," and "you are my witnesses." The poem clearly does not make a metaphysical appeal, but depends on the dramatic effectiveness of the claim enacted and substantiated in court. The cruciality of the witnesses for the future of the world, as the world of Yahweh or as the world of some other god, is inescapable. Indeed, pains are taken

---

97 See, negatively, v. 9 on the failed witnesses of the failed gods.

to discredit other witnesses (41:24b; 44:9) as a means of discrediting the god-claims they voice. The dramatic, courtroom location of Israel proceeds with a recognition that "what is" (*reality*) effectively derives from "what is said" (*testimony*). Testimony leads reality and makes a decision for a certain kind of reality both possible and inescapable.

The two scenarios of Joshua 24 and Isaiah 43 are, *mutatis mutandis*, paradigmatic in every generation and every circumstance for those who engage in the God-talk modeled here. Which witnesses are believed—concerning Yahweh or the gods "beyond the River and in Egypt"—will determine the internal shape of the community. Which witnesses are believed—concerning Yahweh or the gods of the empire—will determine the shape of the world. Testimony to this particular, peculiar God, voiced in ways that are as odd as the God to which witness is borne, is characteristically offered from a position of vulnerability. This vulnerability, however, is not evidence against its veracity. The testimony is neither reductionist nor coercive. It is given in all its elusiveness and density, and then the witnesses await the decision of the court, while other testimony is given by other witnesses for other gods. The waiting is long and disconcerting, because witnesses to other gods are sometimes most formidable. And the jury only trickles in—here and there, now and then.